WORLD BANKING
AND
FINANCE

WORLD BANKING AND FINANCE

Cooperation Versus Conflict

George Macesich

PRAEGER SPECIAL STUDIES • PRAEGER SCIENTIFIC

New York • Philadelphia • Eastbourne, UK
Toronto • Hong Kong • Tokyo • Sydney

Library of Congress Cataloging in Publication Data

Macesich, George, Date-
    World banking and finance.

    Includes index
    1. Banks and banking, International. 2. Inter-
national finance. 3. Debts, External—Developing
countries. 4. Game theory. I. Title.
HG3881.M234 1984   332.1'5   84-17908
ISBN 0-03-001397-6 (alk. paper)

Published in 1984 by Praeger Publishers
CBS Educational and Professional Publishing,
a Division of CBS Inc.
521 Fifth Avenue, New York, NY 10175 USA

456789 052 987654321

Printed in the United States of America
on acid-free paper

In Memory of
My Uncle

GEORGE (DJURO) TEPAVAC

PREFACE

This study examines the underlying forces of change in world banking and the ongoing dialogue between developing-debtor countries and developed-creditor countries within the framework of a theory of cooperation. The basic framework is the theory of cooperation and reflects the evidence provided by recent studies and history.

It draws upon computer tournaments of the Prisoner's Dilemma from game theory and how cooperation evolves. The study draws especially on the work of Robert Axelrod and William D. Hamilton and the implications of their studies for the theory of cooperation. By means of a computer tournament Axelrod studied the ways cooperation evolved. He was able to perceive the underlying principles and prove theories that established the facts and conditions of the rise of cooperation out of nothing. Subsequently he and Hamilton worked out the implications of these discoveries for evolutionary theory.

This book considers and extends the implications of their discoveries for relations between developing-debtor and developed-creditor nations. These relations can best be described as an area where independent, egoistic nations face each other in a state of near anarchy. Can developed and developing countries evolve reliable cooperative strategies? Can cooperation emerge in a world of sovereign states? In short, can cooperation evolve out of noncooperation? Specifically, how can cooperation get started at all? Can cooperation strategies survive better than their rivals? Which cooperative strategies will do best, and how will they come to predominate? The principal conclusion of the study is that cooperation can indeed work with an appropriate strategy. It turns out that the appropriate strategy is a simple Tit for Tat strategy submitted to Axelrod by Anatol Rapoport with the first move being cooperation.

World banks can and do serve as instruments (or clusters) for promoting a Tit for Tat strategy of cooperation. The large debt owed by developing nations to their developed-nation creditors including banks can serve to enhance cooperation among nations. It can promote the evolution of an international environment in which a strategy of cooperation will displace egoistic strategies. And world debt is now of a size that assures cooperators the necessary cluster for a strategy of cooperation to be firmly established. Once established it will tend to flourish as in an ecologically evolving world reported by Axelrod and Hamilton. It is indeed an opportunity for the world to move up the ratchet of cooperation as the theory of cooperation suggests.

The book weaves together institutional and theoretical and empirical results of game theory, computer simulation, monetary theory, and policy analysis so that each reinforces the other. Only when many strands are woven together can we have a useful understanding of the ongoing dialogue between developing-debtor countries and developed-creditor countries and the changing anatomy of world banking and its significance to the world economy. It is directed to the general economist, political scientist, banker, and layman. I hope that it may have some influence in moving toward that consensus of views that our understanding and approach to the vexatious problems of cooperation between developing-debtor countries and developed-creditor countries is enhanced by the fact that mutual cooperation can indeed emerge without central control by starting with a cluster of units which rely on reciprocity. The process of trial and error in dealing with such global issues as banking and world debt is slow and painful. The conditions for cooperation and mutually rewarding strategies based on reciprocity are there.

I am indebted to many colleagues with whom I have discussed one or another aspect of the study. These include especially Marshall R. Colberg, Walter Macesich, Jr., Anna J. Schwartz, Dimitrije Dimitrijević, Branimir M. Janković, Rikard Lang, Dragomir Vojnić and Ljubisav Marković. I should also like to express appreciation for editorial assistance from Grace Colberg and for efficient and helpful typing services to Clydeyne Nelson.

GEORGE MACESICH

CONTENTS

LIST OF TABLES AND FIGURES

TABLES

FIGURES

1.

WORLD ECONOMY AND A
THEORY OF COOPERATION

THE DEBT PROBLEM

The sharp disinflation from 1979-83 forced a series of wrenching changes in the structure of the world economy. This disinflation transition represents the most radical disturbance that has hit the world economy since World War II. As a result of human action but not human intention we did not have Milton Friedman's well known monetarist policy of gradualism, but the more publicized central bank variety of a series of sharp shocks.

The falling tide of inflation has left aground many developing-debtor countries, some of whom had guessed wrong on inflation, with more than $600 billion in foreign debt owed, for the most part, to the world banks of developed-creditor countries.[1] To refloat these countries will require financial statesmanship by banks, domestic monetary authorities, as well as bank examining authorities, and the International Monetary Fund (IMF) together with the cooperation of developing-debtor countries.

World banks, including U.S. banks, that participated in the lending to the developing-debtor countries are primarily responsible for the debt problem, but it would be unrealistic to suggest that the bank examining authorities of developed-creditor countries responsible for appraising the soundness of loans and investments of the banks have lived up to their responsibilities. In the United States the Comptroller's office, with the Federal Deposit Insurance Corporation (FDIC), examines the national banks; the state member

1

banks are examined by state authorities as well as federal agencies and the FDIC. Instead of criticizing these loans, many governments and the IMF are suggesting that banks increase their present exposure.

The problem can be solved and it involves changes in the present policies that would involve a continuing role for banks. It does not mean the monetization of bad debts, nor providing capital and loans to support and refloat stranded developing-debtor nations without their casting over the side excess cargo of misguided and misdirected programs. For instance, the key to cutting fuel and food imports without cutting growth in these countries lies in the greater use of the price mechanism.

Indeed the World Bank in its Sixth World Development Report underscores that developing countries can curb oil imports without permanently slowing their growth by raising their domestic prices in tune with world prices. Not many did so after the oil shock of 1973-74. The argument for not doing so was that oil was essential to growth. The 1979-80 oil shock forced them to cut back on subsidies to fuel. To their surprise, growth did not suffer permanent damage thanks to better and more efficient fuel uses dictated by higher relative prices for oil.

Even bigger input saving can be achieved in agriculture and the food industry. By raising agricultural prices, some developing-debtor nations have found fewer people moving into overcrowded cities. The spending power of the majority of people is increased while at the same time less food needs to be imported and the whole economy benefits.

The legitimate needs of the developing-debtor countries can be met with increasing levels of international trade and continued decrease in unemployment. It is, however, incumbent upon these countries to set their own houses in order without imposing the thankless task onto the IMF for telling them to do so. Misplaced ideological rhetoric for instance against equity investments and related issues are but cases in point. In highly interdependent world capital markets such a strategy serves only to punish its practitioner. In effect, developing-debtor countries must see more to the "supply-side" of their economies, using this term for once in its correct sense.

All of this will require diplomacy — the process of eliminating or reducing conflict through reflection, talk, and bargaining — which is now more valuable than ever in dealing with the global debt issue.

Diplomacy permits — demands, if one is serious — genuine exchange of views. Diplomacy allows one to find out the other country's needs, which may turn out to be compatible with one's own. Diplomacy's give and take tests the importance of one's own country's needs. Successful diplomacy leaves in its wake good relations, mutual trust, and hope for better times. It is not a failure of will for developed-creditor countries to listen to those countries that are weaker, or even hostile. We usually honor that quality when we see it in private life. Moreover, the debt issue and the growing fear of protectionism has already changed the terms of their dialogue with the strong.

Some accords are imperfect — such is the nature of compromise and human affairs generally. Some were lucky rather than skillful achievements — such are among the happy contingencies of diplomacy. And some happened because a country was ready to retaliate in kind — such retaliation is a useful reserve, as we shall see, for those occasions when the other party insists on a course of action irrespective of the consequences on anyone else.

This study presents and discusses a theory of cooperation with reciprocity and a strategy for its implementation as one way of dealing with the global debt problem. In our theory, world banks play an important role owing to their unique characteristics. For instance, large world banks, unlike many of the smaller banks, have a long standing relationship with a given country which enables them to take a longer-term view when dealing with their foreign clients. They tend, moreover, to have less of an incentive to declare a default on loans. Many of these foreign loans are unsecured foreign government loans and/or guaranteed by a foreign government. As a result debt servicing may be interrupted but most, not necessarily all, loans are eventually repaid.[2]

It may not be necessary to undertake a massive refunding operation nor a mandatory transfer of bank claims to a new international organization, nor even a systematic stretching out of existing maturities. Consistent with our theory, for example, would be a more automatic supply of short-term liquidity by the Bank for International Settlements (BIS) and the IMF, and creation of a market for bank claims with some official support by central banks. A system of partial guarantees by multilateral world institutions, not by national governments, to help commercial banks make new loan commitments and adequate surveillance by the IMF so as to ensure that new lending will support sound economic policies are also methods which would be consistent with our theory of cooperation.

This does not mean that developing-debtor nations will be relieved from dealing with long-term problems related to the structural aspects of the debt crisis — essential problems with great social implications and effects on employment and population, on natural resources and energy, on innovation and capital formation. Similar structural problems face many of the developed-creditor countries as well. But if developed-creditor nations are able to maintain monetary stability and avoid inflation, to forbid themselves the use of protectionist measures, and to view the debt issue in proper perspective as an opportunity for promoting world cooperation, the world will be the better for it.

ROLE OF BANKS

World banks in their lending activities have managed to transfer significant resources from the developed to developing countries. As a result they may have provided the world with a mechanism whereby a strategy of cooperation based on reciprocity can gain a foothold in an otherwise iterated Prisoner's Dilemma[3] game which the developed and developing countries play out on the world scene.

Clearly banks did not have such a result in mind — again a result of human action if not human intention. They have more at risk in the current international debt crisis, which has every indication of continuing for many years, than any other sector of the economy. In the scramble for market share, these banks set a pattern of lend first and ask questions later. If opportunity knocked, they opened the door. If regulators stood in the way, the banks challenged them. In the process they are changing the anatomy of world banking and providing the world with a rare opportunity for constructive cooperation.

Here is a good example of the endogenous unplanned aspect of social institutions which is counter to the usual social-scientific view of institutions as planned or designed mechanisms given exogenously to the theorist. It is Nobel Laureate F. A. Hayek who suggests research into the unplanned or unconscious interaction of social agents in order to investigate the spontaneous or unintended social institutions they create.[4] Indeed, it is a major theme of Hayek's social philosophy that emergent or spontaneous outcomes, or more descriptively, the unintended consequences of human action are both efficient and desirable.[5] In our example the market place is finding ways to accomplish changes in banking and the world economy without the benefit of conscious action by government.

This study examines the underlying forces of change in world banking and of the on-going dialogue between developing-debtor countries and developed-creditor countries within the context of a theory of cooperation. It argues that these forces are best understood by drawing on theory, history, and comparative experience in the United States and other countries. The study thus weaves together institutional, theoretical, and empirical results of monetary theory, game theory, computer simulation, and policy analysis so that each reinforces the others. It is only when many strands are woven together that we can have a useful understanding of the on-going dialogue between developing-debtor countries and developed-creditor countries and the changing anatomy of world banking and its significance to the world economy.

DEVELOPING AND DEVELOPED COUNTRY DIALOGUE

The status of the dialogue between developing and developed countries is suggested by the Sixth U.N. Conference on Trade and Development (UNACTAD VI) held in Belgrade, Yugoslavia in June, 1983. The conference addressed itself to a number of continuing problems if not to their solutions. The conference, between the world's "rich and poor" ended in frustration. To be sure in terms of mere dialogue — more gentle persuasion and less fist banging — the conference was generally rated a success. For the first time the conference benefited from no visible confrontation.

This change in tactics and subsequent lack of polemical debate is deceptive. The conference showed that the industrialized North and developing South are no closer to bridging the economic divide that lies between them.

The poor nations want billions of dollars from the richer nations to refloat their economies marooned by the economic downturn of 1979-83. This downturn has left 94 of the 125 developing countries represented in the conference saddled with debt amounting to about $626 billion at the end of 1982.

What they received were minor concessions. They were offered no fresh financial commitments nor did they win approval for a doubling of quotas to the International Monetary Fund which assists countries with balance of payment difficulties. The major industrial countries did agree to try to halt protectionism by sticking to stand-still provisions, but they fell short of their demand for a rollback of protectionist measures. On commodities, the third-world countries failed to carry the United States along with them on a conference resolution to ratify the common fund to boost low commodity prices.

Some observers of the UNCTAD VI Conference argue that it stumbled because of a problem of perceptions.[6] I agree. Thus the rich countries at first assumed that since the poor nations were adopting a conciliatory rather than confrontational stance, it signaled a moderation in the actual substance of their platform. It did not.

The poor countries, in truth, misinterpreted the endorsement by the rich nations of their more moderate attitude as a sign of consensus that the two sides would move forward on the actual specifics of the third world package. As it turned out, they were wrong.

The participants were simply operating on different wave lengths. Central to everything, however, was what had produced the 1979-83 world economic downturn and what measures should be taken to remedy it.

The developed countries largely view the problem as cyclical. In short, as recovery takes hold the benefits will trickle down to the developing countries. Their export prices will go up and they will be able to pay their debts.

As a result the developed nations persist in their cyclical view of world economic downturn. They will not risk upsetting an economic recovery by injecting additional liquidity through a new allocation of special drawing rights (central bank reserves created by the IMF) or adjusting existing financial institutions such as the IMF or the World Bank.

The view of the developing countries is simply opposite. They view the world problems as structural, not cyclical. They do not hold with the trickle-down theory, and are convinced that even if there is a recovery, another recession will only put them back in the economic hole out of which they are now trying to climb.

The remedy, then, is a redistribution of world resources and a revamping of the global economic system that they say discriminates against them.

It is important to understand at the outset that lending and borrowing nations have profited greatly from the trade activity fueled by the loans of world banks. That trade has woven a fabric of interdependence that we tamper with only at our peril.

Development in third world countries is vitally intertwined with bank lending. There is, of course, room for disagreement as to whether it was possible for government, bankers, regulators, and others to have foreseen the depth of the recession of 1979-83 before excess lending occurred. Energy problems and the recycling of petrodollars unleashed a unilateral transfer of wealth to oil-producing countries and pushed the international financial markets into a state of turmoil that later was aggravated by the worldwide recession.

Countries have met the energy problem in one of three ways. The United States tried to protect current consumption to the detriment of the future stock of capital. The Japanese cut consumption. And countries like Brazil, Mexico, Yugoslavia, and others found it very difficult to do as the Japanese did, so they borrowed. Their debt increased rapidly, and the recession's weakening of world markets along with exchange rate volatility, made repayment all the more difficult.

More important, perhaps, is what the third world countries would look like politically, economically and socially if they had not borrowed? In short, what are the results of the unintended actions taken for the most part by the world's banks in their own behalf and in their interest?

A case in point is Brazil with an outstanding debt of almost $100 billion. In 1964, Brazil began reforming and stabilizing its economy, leading to policies of high industrial growth. Energized by infusions of foreign loan capital and direct investment from 1968 to 1973, the Brazilian economy galloped along at an annual growth rate of over 11 percent.

Countries like Brazil, as we noted, were hit hard by the OPEC events of 1973. Their planners saw a need for massive investments in hydroelectric and other energy related projects to lessen vulnerability to imported oil. In today's markets those decisions could be questioned. In tomorrow's, perhaps not.

Brazil's growth did slacken to about 6 percent in the late 1970s, yet even that pace more than matched the long-term growth levels in the industrialized countries.

Another illustration is South Korea. In 1962, manufacturing accounted for less than 16 percent of GNP; after ten years of heavy investment that figure jumped to 36 percent. During the first half of that period, economic growth averaged about 8 percent. Then, during a period when external bank lending became more pronounced, the growth rate climbed to almost 12 percent, where it stood for several years. Major financial reforms sharply increased the intermediary role of banks in private capital markets to support a major spurt of industrialization.

And in Yugoslavia after a significant slowing down of the rate of increase in GMP (gross material product) following the 1965 Reform from 8.6 percent in 1953-64 to 5.5 percent in 1965-70, the rate of increase in GMP rose to nearly 6 percent in the 1970s. This is more than six times higher than the rate of growth of population (.9 percent annual rate).[7] The second characteristic of the rate of economic development in this period is the variability of the rate of growth of GMP from a high of 8.6 percent in 1974 to a low of 3.1 percent in 1980 and 2.0 percent in 1981. Starting from a rather low level in the 1940s, per capita GMP reached $2,486 at the end of the 1970s. Translated into GNP (gross national product) it is about 15 percent higher, about $2,860. Compared with European countries at a similar level of economic development, the per capita GNP of Yugoslavia is higher than those of Portugal, ($2,180) and Turkey ($1,160) but lower than those of Greece ($3,960) and Spain (more than $5,000).

Though many factors are necessary for growth in the developing countries, it is clear almost by definition of a developing country that only a small portion of the financing can be generated by internal savings.

In addition to direct lending to third world countries, development moves forward by means of investment by transnational companies. To an important extent, that investment is mobilized by bank lending.

As for the industrial countries a kind of double recycling has taken place: as funds invested in local projects begin raising incomes, markets develop that generate jobs and export revenues for the industrial countries. In the case of the United States, exports make up an evergrowing proportion of the economy. Indeed over 40 percent of American exports now go to third world countries.

For their part many banks are still making significant profits. Thus in Britain the big four clearing banks' profits in the first half of 1982 were significantly greater than in 1980. American banks registered a 5 to 10 percent increase in profits in 1982 over 1981.

Most banks in the United States and elsewhere are thus in reasonable shape. They have built up provisions over the years against the possibility of having sometime in the future to write off a loan. Their continuing ability to do so, however, depends on the economic cycle.

Bank losses lag behind economic cycles because enterprises do not always collapse at once but do so over time, bolstering themselves for as long as possible with more short-term bank debt. The severity of the post-1979 economic decline has underscored the cyclical factor. For instance one report notes that Britain's Midland Bank had, in 1982, 70 medium-to-large companies in its unit with debts of around £350 million.[8]

The nonperforming assets (so-called because interest is not being paid) of large American money center banks has increased significantly over the cycle, however they are still less than they were in 1970. Such large disasters as Chrysler and International Harvester in the United States, A.E.G. in Germany, and Massey-Ferguson in Canada occur slowly. Still, during the past economic contraction, corporate bankruptcies in America were at record levels. Business failures in Britain were up 35 percent in 1982. In Canada, banks' 1982 losses on loans exceeded those in 1981.

Bank insolvency and threatened world banking collapse, nevertheless, did not take place. Provisions provided by banks for bad loans are also supplemented by bank capital. The ratios of capital to assets have been improving, especially in the case of large American banks by comparison to recent years. These are the banks with considerable exposure overseas.

The hidden reserves of German and Swiss banks have absorbed large losses without significant damage to their balance sheets. Indeed, observers note that the recent crises in these two countries has strengthened the argument for hidden reserves.

A THEORY OF COOPERATION

If the market place is finding ways to accomplish changes in banking and the world economy without the benefit of conscious action by planners and governments, relations between developed and developing countries can be described as an area where independent, egoistic nations face each other in a state of near anarchy. Can developed and developing countries evolve reliable cooperative strategies? Can cooperation emerge in a world of sovereign states? In short, can cooperation evolve out of noncooperation? Specifically, how can cooperation get started at all? Can cooperation strategies survive better than their rivals? Which cooperative strategies will do best, and how will they come to predominate?

Many of the problems facing these nations take the form of an iterated Prisoner's Dilemma.[9] In the Prisoner's Dilemma game two individuals (or nations) can either cooperate or defect. The payoff to a player is in terms of the effect in terms of the payoff. No matter what the other does, the selfish choice of defection yields a higher payoff than cooperation. But, if both defect, both do worse than if both had cooperated.

For purposes of illustration let us assume that A (developed-creditor nations) and B (developing-debtor nations) in Figure 1.1 agree to trade. Both are satisfied as to the amounts they will be

FIGURE 1.1
Prisoner's Dilemma. (A = Developed/Creditor Nations; B = Developing Debtor Nations; the game is defined by: $T > R > P > S$ and $R > (S+T)/2$.)

Nations A	Nations B	
C Cooperation	R = 3,3 Mutual Cooperation	S = 0,5 Sucker's Payoff
D Defection	T = 5,0 Temptation to Defect	P = 1,1 Punishment for Mutual Defection

receiving. Assume further that for some reason the exchange is to take place in secret. Both agree to place money in a designated location. Let us also assume that neither A nor B will ever meet again nor have further dealings.

Now if both A and B carry out their agreement both stand to gain. It is also obvious that if neither A nor B carried out the agreement neither would have what it wanted. It is equally obvious if only one carried out its end of the bargain, say A, B would receive something for nothing, since they will never again meet nor have further dealings. There is thus an incentive for both A and B to leave nothing. As a result neither A nor B get what they initially wanted. Does the logic prevent cooperation? That is the Prisoner's Dilemma.

The iterated Prisoner's Dilemma can be made more quantitative and in that form studied by the methods of game theory and computer simulation. In order to do this we build a *pay off matrix* presenting hypothetical values for the various alternatives such as in Figure 1.1.

In this matrix mutual cooperation by A and B yields to both parties 3 points. Mutual defection yields to both 0 points. If A cooperates but B does not, B gets 5 points because it is better to get something for nothing. The number 3 is called the *reward for cooperation* R. The number 1 is called the *punishment* or P. The number 5 is T for *temptation*, and 0 is S, the *sucker's payoff*. The conditions necessary for the matrix to represent a Prisoner's Dilemma are the following:

$$T > R > S. \qquad (1.1)$$

$$T + S < R. \qquad (1.2)$$

2

The first condition (1.1) says that it is better to defect no matter what the other side does. The second condition (1.2) in effect guarantees that if A and B get locked into an out of phase alteration, for example, A cooperates but B defects in one period and B cooperates but A defects in the second period, A will not do better. In fact A will do worse than if A cooperated in each period.

If A and B will never meet again (an unlikely situation in our example) the only appropriate solution indicated by the game is to defect always. This strategy is correct even though both could do better if they cooperated. Thus in the case of Prisoner's Dilemma played only once, to defect is always the best strategy.

In the case of our iterated Prisoner's Dilemma game where the same two participants may meet more than once, a much greater set of options is available. Strategy would include a decision rule which determines the probability of cooperation or defection as a formation of the history of interaction thus far. However, if there is a known number of interactions between a pair of individuals, to defect always is still evolutionarily stable (for example, individuals using the strategy of defection can not do better by another strategy). The reason is that the defection on the last interaction would be optional for both sides. And, of course, so would defection on the next to the last interaction and on back to the first.

On the other hand if the number of interactions is not fixed in advance, but given by some probability, W, that after the first interaction the same two individuals (nations) will meet again, other strategies become evolutionarily stable as well. Indeed when W is sufficiently great, there is no single best strategy regardless of the behavior of the other in the population. The matter, however, is not hopeless.

In fact, Axelrod and Hamilton demonstrate that there is a strategy that is stable, robust, and viable. Accordingly, evolution of cooperation can be conceptualized in terms of three separate questions:

1. *Robustness*. What type of strategy can thrive in a variegated environment composed of others using a wide variety of more or less sophisticated strategies?
2. *Stability*. Under what conditions can such a strategy, once fully established, resist invasion by mutant strategies?
3. *Initial viability*. Even if a strategy is robust and stable, how can it ever get a foothold in an environment which is predominately noncooperative?[10]

The authors submitted various strategies to a computer tournament drawing upon contributors in game theory from economics, mathematics, political science and sociology. The result of the tournament was that "the highest average score was attained by the simplest of all strategies submitted: Tit for Tat. This strategy is simply one of cooperating on the first move and then doing what the other player did on the preceding move. Thus Tit for Tat is a strategy of cooperation based on reciprocity."[11]

The robustness of Tit for Tat is reported by the authors as dependent on three features: "it was never the first to defect, it was provocable into retaliation by a defection of the other, and it was forgiving after just one act of retaliation . . . in the long run, Tit for Tat displaced all other rules and went to fixation . . ." and so provides ". . . further evidence that Tit for Tat's cooperation based on reciprocity is a robust strategy that can thrive in a variegated environment."[12]

The authors then demonstrate that once Tit for Tat has gone to fixation it can resist invasion by any possible mutant strategy provided that individuals who interact have a sufficiently large probability, W, of meeting again.

Since Tit for Tat is not the only strategy that can be evolutionarily stable, it raises the problem of how an evolutionary trend to cooperative behavior could ever have started in the first place. Axelrod and Hamilton provide several illustrations where benefits of cooperation can be harvested by groups of closely related individuals.

Clustering can also lead to a Tit for Tat strategy even when virtually everyone is using an all D (Defection) strategy. Suppose that a small group of individuals is using Tit for Tat and that a certain proportion, p, of the interactions of the members of the cluster are with other members of the cluster. Then the average score attained by members of the cluster using Tit for Tat strategy is

$$p[R/(1-w)] + (1-p)[S+W \cdot P/(1-w)]. \qquad (1.3)$$

If the members of the cluster provide a negligible proportion of the interactions for the other individuals, then the score attained by those using all D is still $P/(1-w)$. When p and w are large enough, a cluster of Tit for Tat individuals can then become initially viable in an environment composed overwhelmingly of all D.

Can the reverse happen? That is, once a strategy of Tit for Tat becomes established can it be displaced? According to the authors the answer is no. This is because the score achieved by the strategy that comes in a cluster is a weighted average of how it does with others of its kind and with the predominant strategy. Each of these components is less than or equal to the score achieved by Tit for Tat. Thus the strategy arriving in a cluster can not intrude on Tit for Tat.

In other words when w is large enough to make Tit for Tat an evolutionarily stable strategy it can resist intrusion by any cluster of any other strategy.

In sum, "cooperation based on reciprocity can get started in a predominantly noncooperative world, can thrive in a variegated environment, and can defend itself once fully established. . . . The gear wheels of social evolution have a ratchet."[13]

It is noteworthy for our purposes that Tit for Tat won the various tournament games not because it managed to beat the other players but by eliciting behavior from the other player that allowed both to do well. Indeed it was so consistent in generating initially rewarding results that it achieved a higher overall score than any other strategy in the tournament.

So-called "non-nice" or tricky strategies designed to sound out how much an opponent "minded" being defected against typically back-fired causing severe breakdowns of trust. In other words, attempts to use defection in a game to "flush out" an opponent's weak spots turns out to be very costly. Indeed, it proved more profitable to have a policy of cooperation as often as possible together with a willingness to retaliate swiftly in a restrained and forgiving manner.

Furthermore straightforwardness and simplicity is the best approach. Being so complex as to be incomprehensible is very dangerous indeed. Too complex a strategy can appear as chaotic. The use of a random strategy can appear as one that is unresponsive to the other player. An unresponsive strategy provides no incentive for the other player to cooperate with you.

The significance of these results for the on-going dialogue between our developing-debtor countries and developed-creditor countries is obvious. It is not surprising that the byzantine strategies followed by some participants in the dialogue have so little to show in the way of concrete results.

Among the important lessons for our developed-developing nations dialogue derived from Axelrod's tournament efforts is that previously game theories did not take their analysis far enough. That is, it is important to minimize echo effects in an environment of mutual power. He argues that a sophisticated analysis calls for going "three levels deep." The first level is the direct effect of a choice. Since a defection always earns more than cooperation, this is easy. The second level is the indirect effect which takes into account that the other side may or may not punish a defection. The effect in the third level is the fact that in responding to the defection of the other side, one may be repeating or even amplifying one's own exploitative choice. Thus a single defection may be successful when considered for its direct effects and perhaps even for its secondary effects. The tertiary effects, however, may be the real costs when one's own single defection turns into unending mutual recriminations. In effect, many of the rules actually wound up punishing themselves, the other player simply serving as a mechanism to delay the self-punishment by a few moves.

In essence, there is a lot to be learned about coping in an environment of mutual power. Indeed, Axelrod reports that many expert strategists from economics, political science, mathematics, sociology, and psychology made the systematic error of being too competitive for their own good, not forgiving enough and too pessimistic about the responsiveness of the other side.

In a nonzero-sum world a nation does not have to do better than another player nation to do well for itself. The more player nations interacting the better. As long as "A" does well it is alright if the others do as well or a little better. It is pointless for "A" to be envious of the success of another country because Prisoner's Dilemma of long duration success over the others is virtually a prerequisite of "A" doing well for itself.

Clearly this principle holds for our debtor and creditor countries. A country that borrows from another can expect that the loan will be mutually beneficial. There is no point in the borrower being envious of the creditor's terms and interest. Any attempt to reduce it through an uncooperative practice, such as not making interest and principal payments on time as agreed, will only encourage the creditor to take retaliatory action. Retaliatory action could take many forms, often without being explicitly labeled as punishment. Poorer credit ratings, less prompt deliveries of needed materials, fewer discounts and in general less favorable market conditions for the debtor country's goods and services. In short, the retaliation could make the loan quite expensive. Instead of worrying about the relative profits of the creditor, the debtor should worry about whether another borrowing strategy would be better. For instance, it can lift domestic restrictions on interest paid on savings and bank deposits thereby mobilizing greater domestic savings which could reduce external borrowing requirements.

The significance of the environment for the endogenous evolution of institutions à la Hayek are the results reported by Axelrod and others in the "ecological tournament".[14] The tournament consists not only of single subjective replay but also of an entire cascade of hypothetical replays, each one's environment determined by the preceding replay. In particular if you take a program's score in a tournament as a measure of its "fitness," and if you interpret fitness to mean "number of progeny in the next generation" and finally if you let next generation mean "next tournament," then what you get is that each tournament's results determine the environment of the next tournament. This type of iterated tournament is called ecological because it stimulates ecological adaptation (the shifting of a fixed set of species populations according to their mutually defined and dynamically developing environment) as contrasted with the mutation-oriented aspects of evolution, where new species can come into existence.

Carrying the ecological tournament generation after generation results in the environment gradually changing. At start both poor and good programs or strategies are equally represented. As the tournament goes on the poorer programs drop out while the good ones remain. The rank order of the good ones now will change since the field of competitors has changed.

In short, success breeds success only if the successful programs are permitted to interact. If, in contrast, the success of some programs is due mostly to their ability to exploit less successful programs, then as these exploit-prone programs are gradually squeezed out, the exploiter's base of support is eroded and it too will bail out, and indeed, as Axelrod points out, playing with rules that do not score well is eventually self-defeating. Not being nice may look promising at the start, but in the long run the effect is to destroy the very environment upon which its success depends.

Consider now the on-going dialogue between developed and developing countries against our theory of cooperation outlined above. Cooperation based on reciprocity can gain a foothold through at least two different mechanisms. One is through *kinship* or closely related individuals and/or institutions. Banks and the debtor-creditor relationship of about $626 billion between developing and developed nations is such a relationship.

A second mechanism to overcome a strategy of total defection (all D) is for the mutant strategy (cooperation) to arrive in such a cluster so that they provide a nontrivial proportion of the inter-action each has. In addition to the $626 billion debt/credit relation-ship between developing and developed nations, the extensive trade relations which now make for increasing world interdependence provides such a cluster.

As reported by Axelrod and Hamilton a computer tournament approach will demonstrate that a strategy of Tit for Tat will fare better than alternative strategies. It is robust. It does well in a variety of circumstances. It is stable and especially against a wide variety of mutant strategies. Cooperation can indeed prosper. It can emerge in a world of egoists without central control by starting with a cluster of individuals/nations who rely on reciprocity.

In short, advice given to players of the Prisoner's Dilemma might also serve world bankers as well as national leaders and others in developing and developed nations in dealing with the current oppor-tunities before the world: Don't be envious, don't be first to defect, reciprocate both defection and cooperation and don't be too clever. These guidelines will serve to gauge various proposals cast up to deal with banking and world economic problems in the following chapters of this book.

To be sure allowance must be made in the application of our Prisoner's Dilemma game to ideology, bureaucratic policies and quality of leadership. Nevertheless, the insights are very useful. Our process of understanding and approach to problems of cooperation is enhanced by the knowledge that mutual cooperation can indeed emerge without central control by starting with a cluster of units which rely on reciprocity. When it is learned that X will lead to Y and Y is felt to be desirable there is an inclination not to prevent Y by not prohibiting X. The process of trial and error in dealing with such global issues as banking and world debt is slow and painful. The conditions for cooperation and mutually rewarding strategies based on reciprocity are there.

Indeed, our theory of cooperation gives added insight into a problem addressed by Mancur Olson — why institutional sclerosis crept up on the West, but at different speeds in different coun-tries.[15] According to Olson the explanation is to be found in the politics and economics of common interest groups and collusive associations. Some strengthen society but others reduce growth, efficiency and the capacity to adapt to outside events. Such "com-mon-interest organizations" tend to prevent or delay changes in relative incomes and prices required when productivity changes or the system is subject to an external shock. Unlike price monopoly however, the influence of the group is not even efficiently wielded. In effect, they are cartelized organizations cautious about change and innovations.

The political consequences are perhaps even more important than the strict economic effects. Interest group lobbying increases the scope and complexity of government. This drains resources to political lobbying, negotiations, and political activity. Individuals with a talent for such activities will be favored over those with strictly technical, entrepreneurial, and other talents. These collusive organizations are expensive to start. Each member has an incentive to be a "free rider" on the actions of others. Participation is costly in terms of fees, lobbying, and time. To be effective, the leadership of such organizations must make it worthwhile for individuals to participate. This may taken the form of pecuniary or nonpecuniary and/or returns moral pressure, or outright coercion. It takes many years for these incentives, pressures, and loyalties to evolve, but once established, interest groups tend to maintain themselves in definitely at much less cost.

Cases in point consistent with Olson's hypothesis are Great Britain which led and promoted the Industrial Revolution and the American industrial heartland. On the other side are cases where concerned interest organizations have for all practical purposes been eliminated by foreign occupation, totalitarian government or political instability. These countries experience rapid rates of growth, according to Olson, after a free and stable legal order is established. The countries of continental Europe in the postwar era are examples.

Eventually many of these common interest organizations again were reestablished in Europe. The use of collective and political pressures and collusive organizations once again made it difficult for countries to react to changed market conditions. For instance, changed market conditions such as those requiring lower real wages are resisted by workers organized into a cartel or lobby, even though advantageous contracts could in principle be made between employers and unemployed workers. The collusive organization with the most power to price workers out of jobs are now the labor unions of Western Europe. In America it is more likely that this power is in the hands of various producer groups including some unions and corporations threatened by imports.

To cast Olson's problem into our theory of cooperation we draw on our discussion of a changing ecological environment. Accordingly, the initial success of some of the common interest groups was due for the most part to their ability to exploit less successful groups. These groups were eventually squeezed out and the exploiter's base of support eroded, thereby destroying the very environment for which its success depended. As we noted, not being nice may look promising at the start but not in the long-run.

The postwar period in Europe and Japan provides additional insights. The Allies reset the tournament according to a new set of rules. The tournament ran well as long as the game was played with good or nice strategies. As we noted, success breeds success only if nice strategies are permitted to interact. The comparatively better performance of Western European countries and Japan on this score stand in marked contrast to that of the East European countries and the Soviet Union. In many East European countries the former common interest groups were replaced but the expected rapid rates of growth did not always materialize thanks to their failure to adopt a nice strategy at the outset. By adopting a non-nice strategy at once some of these countries destroyed the environment much more quickly, than others in Westen Europe. Even so reinstitution of a nice strategy with its concomitant positive influence on the environment is still possible in these countries through economic and political reforms which some have undertaken.

NOTES

1. The seriousness of the debt crisis can be dated from Friday, August 13, 1982, when Mexico announced that it was no longer able to service $80 billion of foreign debts. In the closing months of 1982 debt rescheduling arrangements were made for Mexico, Brazil, Argentina, and other countries.

2. Unlike a domestic firm, a foreign country *may* not become insolvent though it can become illiquid. The qualification is necessary because regimes and dynasties come and go in countries and not all pay their debts as many a foreign bond holder has learned to his sorrow. The *capacity* and *willingness* to repay are not necessarily identical.

3. First formulated in about 1950 by Merril M. Flood and Melvin Dresher and later formulized by Albert W. Tucker, according to Douglas R. Hofstadter, "Metamagical Themas: Computer Tournaments of the Prisoner's Dilemma Suggest How Cooperation Evolves," *Scientific American* May, 1983. pp. 16-23. Prisoner's Dilemma derives its name from a game which has no satisfactory

solution, that is, whatever choice is recommended by "Rational Considerations," has something wrong with it in spite of the fact that nothing remains unknown about the situation. In other words, the chooser cannot do better by finding out more; hence the dilemma.

4. F. A. Hayek, *The Counterrevolution in Science* (New York: Free Press, 1955). See also Andrew Schotter, *The Economic Theory of Social Institutions* (Cambridge: Cambridge University Press, 1981) and Martin Shubik, "A Theory of Money and Financial Institutions: Fiat Money and Noncooperative Equilibrium in a Closed Economy" *International Journal of Game Theory*, 1971/ 1972, 7 (1), pp. 243-68.

5. F. A. Hayek, *The Constitution of Liberty* (Chicago: Henry Regnery Co., 1960); F. A. Hayek, *Law, Legislation and Liberty* Vol. 1, *Rules and Order* (Chicago: University of Chicago Press, 1973); and Vol. 2 *Mirage of Social Justice* (Chicago: University of Chicago Press, 1976). To be sure Hayek's view of the endogenous nature of institutions takes place within a specified environment: namely, one where general rules are adhered to. The environment guarantees that only efficient institutions orders-outcomes will emerge. See Roger A. Arnold, "Hayek and Institutional Evolution," *The Journal of Libertarian Studies* Vol. IV, No. 4, Fall 1980. pp. 341-52.

6. See for instance, David Winder "Talks between rich and poor nations end in frustration." *The Christian Science Monitor* July 7, 1983, p. 7.

7. See Rikard Lang, George Macesich, and Dragomir Vojnić (ed.) *Essays on the Political Economy of Yugoslavia since 1974* (Zagreb: Informator, 1982); Dimitrije Dimitrijević and George Macesich, *Money and Finance in Yugoslavia: A Comparative Analysis* (New York: Praeger Publishers, 1984); *Proceedings and Reports* vols. 9-16, (Tallahassee: Center for Yugoslav Studies, Research and Exchanges. Florida State University, 1971-1982).

8. *The Economist* October 16, 1982. p. 26.

9. Robert Axelrod and William D. Hamilton, "The Evolution of Cooperation" *Science*, March 27, 1981, pp. 1390-96; Douglas R. Hofstadter "Metamagical Themas" *Scientific American*, May, 1983, pp. 16-26; Anton Rapoport and A. M. Chammah, *Prisoner's Dilemma* (Ann Arbor: University of Michigan Press, 1965); D. Luce and H. Raiffa, *Games and Decisions* (New York: John Wiley and Sons, 1975) pp. 94-102; M. Cohen, T. Nagel, and T. Scanlon (eds.) *War and Moral Responsibility* (Princeton: Princeton University Press, 1974); B. Belassa and R. Nelson (eds.) *Economic Progress, Private Values and Public Policy: Essays in Honor of William Felner* (Amsterdam: North-Holland Publishing Company, 1977); M. Taylor, *Anarchy and Cooperation* (New York: John Wiley and Sons, 1976); Robert Axelrod, *Evolution of Cooperation* (New York: Basic Books, 1984); Andrew Schotter, *The Economic Theory of Social Institutions* (Cambridge: Cambridge University Press, 1981); Andrew Schotter and Gerhard Schwödiauer, "Economics and the Theory of Games: A Survey" *Journal of Economic Literature*, June, 1980, pp. 479-527.

10. Axelrod and Hamilton op. cit., p. 1393.

11. Ibid., p. 1393 The strategy of Tit for Tat was submitted to the tournament by Professor Anatol Rapoport, a psychologist and philosopher at the University of Toronto.

12. Ibid. an all D (Defection) strategy.

13. Ibid., 1394.

14. The discussion in the following two paragraphs draws on Douglas R. Hofstadter op. cit., pp. 24-25.

15. Mancur Olson, *The Rise and Decline of Nations* (New Haven: Yale University Press, 1982).

2.

WORLD DEBT AND THE BANKS

A LOOK AT THE EVIDENCE

The debt can be viewed as a blessing in disguise. It can serve to enhance cooperation among the developing-debtor countries and developed-creditor countries. It can promote the evolution of an international environment in which a strategy of cooperation will displace egoistic strategies. And world debt is now of a size that assures cooperators the necessary cluster for a strategy of cooperation to be firmly established. Once established it will tend to flourish as in an ecologically evolving world.

Just how large is the world debt and how was it acquired? It is larger than previously thought and not always prudently acquired. To judge from the results of a survey by the Paris-based Organization for Economic Cooperation and illustrated in Table 2.1, developing countries owe $626 billion in middle and long-term external debt in 1982 up from $530 billion at the end of 1981. The latter figure is more comprehensive than the $465 billion cited by the World Bank for the end of 1981.

The study estimates that between mid-1982 and the end of 1983, developing countries may have to reschedule into longer-term debt some $15 billion of short-term debt they owe commercial banks. The bulk of this rescheduled recovery will be owed by Latin American nations. The survey cautions, however, that there is considerable uncertainty as to the size of shortfalls in current debt-service payments by certain debtors in Latin America. In fact, the study was

TABLE 2.1
How Much Developing Countries Owe Their Creditors: Total Debt at Year-end and Annual Repayments, Including Interest Changes (billions of dollars)

	1971	'78	'80	'81*	'82†
Industrial countries and capital markets					
Total	71	266	361	407	476
Each year	9.2	51.7	75.8	95.9	115.2
Bank loans as percentage of industrial Country loans					
Total	15.5	39.2	42.9	44.2	44.1
Each year	n.a.	47.6	50.3	51.7	48.6
Multilateral organizations, such as					
World Bank, Asian Development Bank, etc.					
Total	10	40	56	65	76
Each year	0.9	3.3	4.8	5.6	6.7
Communist countries					
Total	6	12	15	17	20
Each year	0.6	1	1	2.1	2.5
OPEC					
Total	0.0	13	18	23	29
Each year	0.0	1.0	1.9	2.4	3.0
Other less developed countries					
Total	2	6	8	10	13
Each year	0.1	0	1.0	1.3	1.9
Other					
Total	1	6	7	8	12
Each year	0.2	1.0	1.7	2.0	2.0
Total debt					
Total	90	345	465	530	626
Each year	11	59	86.9	109.3	131.3

*Preliminary
†Estimate
n.a. = Not available

Source: Organization for Economic Cooperation and Development; and The Christian Science Monitor, December 17, 1982 pp. 11.

probably put together before the seriousness of Brazil's debt problems became so evident.

Other facts noted in the survey include: Excluding short-term debt, during 1978-81 renegotiated debt service to private banks represented on average less than 3 percent of total debt-service due by the developing countries and about 6 percent of debt-service obligations due to banks.

Particularly during the past four or five years, debt-service payments have increased rapidly. They have reached an estimated $131 billion in 1982 with interest payments accounting for $60 billion and amortization payments for $71 billion.

The annual nominal interest costs on fixed-interest debt (medium and long term) rose moderately between 1972 and 1982, from 5 to 7.9 percent. On floating interest debt — essentially Euro-currency debt — interest increased sharply from 7.8 to 17.5 percent. The OECD study expected a marked decline in 1983 owing to a declining London Interbank Bank Offer Rate (LIBOR). The average interest rate on all types of outstanding debt climbed to 11.3 percent in 1982.

Indeed, the OECD economists argue that as a result of the debt problem the financial structure created over the past decade is wobbly. As for the reason, it is certainly true that some developing countries have borrowed unwisely "using some of the resources to finance consumption and investments of dubious value, rather than to strengthen their productive potential . . . overeagerness by banks to lend has sometimes allowed borrowing governments to delay necessary adjustments."[1]

It is also true, however, that many developing countries borrowed abroad because of the failure and/or lack of adequate domestic banking and financial institutions to marshal domestic savings and to allocate such savings productively. In good part, the responsibility is with the governments of these countries. All too often they have failed to create with proper incentives the necessary domestic financial intermediaries and/or eliminated nascent financial institutions and markets for vague and often ideological reasons.

Banks in the industrial countries have often been forced into riskier foreign ventures as a result of attempts to evade archaic restrictions imposed on their domestic operations by government. A case in point in the United States was the Federal Reserve System's Regulation Q which places a limit on the rate of interest U.S. banks were allowed to pay on deposits received at their offices in the United States. As the nominal rates of interest rose during the inflationary 1960s and 1970s, U.S. banks were restrained by Regulation Q ceilings from paying domestic depositors interest rates that could compete with interest return from alternative financial instruments, such as U.S. government Treasury bills and short-term unsecured promissory notes issued by large U.S. corporations. Banks experienced a run-off in deposits at domestic offices because of their inability to compete effectively for domestic funds. To supplement their traditional sources of funds, U.S. banks found it expedient to turn to their foreign branches that were not subject to interest rate ceilings and, thus, were free to compete for funds. Deposits taken in at overseas branches were transferred back to the United States for use by the domestic offices. They also increased their loan exposures in developing countries attracted by higher returns and in most cases encouraged by their governments.

In recycling OPEC dollars banks allowed themselves a sizable spread in terms of returns. The largest American money-center banks as a group emerged as the largest supporters of credit to country borrowers and indirectly to the interbank system. One observer notes that surplus funds from the treasuries of the large American banks were made available to smaller banks or foreign banks unable to attract deposits directly denominated in foreign currency.[2] These other banks in turn used the money to lend to the same community of borrowers. As a result exposure of the big American banks was ensured through the inter-bank markets even when loans were extended by other banks. The point is that once funds are channeled through the interbank markets there is no control over their end use. The same is true for other large European and Japanese banks.

Monetary activities in the United States did little to discourage such developments. There is no reason at that time why they should have. The intermediation was taking place in the market as a result of the interplay of supply and demand. Indeed the Federal Reserve viewed American bank participation in the recycling process as a tool of the strength of American policy.

Again the large European and Japanese banks played their part. Indeed, non-American banks conducting their operations through the Euromarkets assumed that if liquidity problems occurred in Euromarkets the American monetary authorities would act as "lenders of last resort." This was a wrong if understandable assumption on their part. They assumed that since the bulk of international debt is denominated in American dollars and American banks have provided the bulk of the funds for the credits, the Federal Reserve will act as lender of last resort if foreign banks cannot meet their liabilities to the American banks. The fact that the Federal Reserve remained silent during the huge expansion of foreign lending by American banks was taken by Europeans and others to be tacit approval.

It was against this background that the world banking community embarked upon a vast credit surge. Thus *The Economist* described the situation where the "Euromarket was seen as the main supplier of money, using net bank deposits as the monetary base. Credit expansion assumed huge proportions, as the modus operandi of the Euromarket came to resemble a Federal Reserve system without reserve requirements or central bank control. Demand rather than supply, dictated its size."[3]

Conditions progressively deteriorated as the average life of loans became shorter and big country borrowers such as Mexico, Brazil, Argentina, Poland, and Yugoslavia saw their total debt concentrated in such short term maturities that it was beyond their ability to service or repay it. The concern was now not only for securing credit for new requirements but with refinancing existing debt due for payment.

How this came to pass is perhaps best described by *The Economist* and merits quotation at length:

> In order to mobilize short-term deposits and credit availability in general, a system was devised whereby lenders entered a commitment to supply money for a given term without having to match it with deposits of comparable maturities. The commitment allowed banks to revise their interest rate periodically (usually at three or six month intervals). As their interest rate was based on the cost of money to themselves plus a spread, the banks could borrow for every interest period and thus refinance the amount they had originally extended to the borrower. . . . At the beginning some efforts were made to apply credit judgment and to justify the purpose of the loan. With time, however, competition among banks to secure a larger share of the business encouraged them to overlook credit-worthiness and even to invent theories to justify an unwise extension of credit. Otherwise — cautious bankers publicly rationalized past action in order to justify the increasing dependence of their institutions on the earnings from their international loans. . . .[4]

Problems for borrowing countries were compounded because "loan maturities had little to do with the actual structure of a country's requirements and loans were put together in terms of size and maturity either to meet market preference or to fit the spread over London Interbank Offered Rate (LIBOR), that borrowers were intending to pay. Though the spread represented an insignificant proportion of the total cost of borrowing, some enterprising bankers − with the help of the press − succeeded in turning it into a credit worthiness rating. Maturities, therefore, had to be shortened in many cases to fit the spread expectations."[5]

This tendency toward short-term financing was reinforced by the idea that a short-term loan was safer than a long-term one "because it would allow that lender to recover his asset before other creditors. Thus, when the market place was reluctant to respond to given requirements, the maturities became shorter to fit the lender's preferences."[6]

At the time when the large surge in lending abroad occurred it was assumed that with time and an expansion in international trade, countries would be able to increase their export earnings and repay their debts. This did not happen for several reasons. In the first place, the size of the debt was inflated by the huge rise in interest rates adding to the cost of servicing the debt. The rise in nominal rates reflected in good part the worldwide inflation. In the second place, attempts to come to grips with inflation by tightening the money supply brought about one of the world's longest postwar recessions. In the third place, as nominal interest rates shot up the cost of new borrowing increased and led to further shortening of maturities and a further increase in the size of loans needed to refinance maturing obligations. Borrowers and their bankers very quickly found themselves concerned mainly with securing continuous financing at any maturity.

By 1982 it became clear that many of the largest world banks were locked into foreign loans in major borrowing countries. The withdrawal of any individual bank from any given country could not only bring about very serious problems for the country concerned, but insolvency for the bank as well. The big banks were thus seriously concerned about their own solvency − that dread wasting disease which is discussed elsewhere. To keep the disease in check they prevailed on other creditors, especially the smaller banks, not to abandon the borrowers. In short, concern over their financial health prompted their monetary authorities to ask all banks to overlook credit worthiness and stick with the borrowers. An absurd position for a central bank to take and perhaps illegal as well, observes *The Economist*,[7] but nevertheless justified in terms of our earlier discussion of a theory of cooperation.

THE EXPOSURE OF BANKS

The exposure of banks to overseas loans is difficult to quantify though it is significant as we noted earlier. According to estimates provided by the *American Banker* and *The Economist*, it is indicated that in 1983 the four largest American banks taken together had outstanding loans which exceeded their equity. Thus Citicorp with a total of $8.7 billion outstanding loans in Brazil, Mexico, and Venezuela registers as 180 percent of the bank's equity; Manufacturers Hanover with $4.8 billion amounts to 174 percent of its equity; Chase Manhattan with $5.1 billion amounts to 183 percent of its equity; Continental Illinois with $1.6 billion amounts to 96 percent of its equity.

Several hundred smaller regional banks in the American south had joined in syndicated loans to Mexico. Some of these banks also made large business and personal loans to Mexico before the imposition of exchange controls and 70 percent devaluation of the Mexican peso. Many doubt that any of these loans will be repaid.

Some idea of American bank exposure in Mexico, for instance, is suggested in Table 2.2. These figures, as reported by *The Economist* December 4, 1982, are third quarter 1982 estimates. They are prepared by the New York broker firm of Smith Barney Harris Upham. They represent an attempt to standardize reports by banks to the Securities Exchange Commission requirement that banks show their loans to troubled countries when they exceed 1 percent of their total assets. These figures do not include compensating balance deposits held by Mexican borrowers with their banks, nor how much has been loaned to the country's private and public sectors.

Indeed some of the American regional banks not listed in Table 2.2 have even bigger shares of their total loans in Mexico. According to *The Economist* and Smith Barney, Arizona's Valley National Bank tops the list with 6.1 percent.

TABLE 2.2
Big American Banks' Mexican Loans Estimated as a Percent of Total Loans
(in percent)

Chemical, New York	4.6
Manufacturers Hanover	3.6
Bank America	3.5
First Chicago	3.5
Bankers Trust	3.4
J. P. Morgan	3.3
Wells Fargo	3.1
Chase Manhattan	2.9
Crocker National	2.9
Citicorp	2.9
First Interstate	2.7
Marine Midland	2.4
Security Pacific	2.1
Continental Illinois	2.0

Source: Smith Barney Harris Upham and *The Economist*, December 4, 1982, p. 80.

High interest rates make repayment of debt more difficult for debtor countries. Estimates are that in Mexico and Brazil each single percentage-point drop in interest rates saves each country around $750 million a year. Although nominal interest rates have come down during the first half of 1983, they remain stubbornly high in real terms and the extra premium many of these countries have to pay has risen significantly. Given their dubious credit ratings, the rates charged these countries may increase as they compete with a revival in demand credit from American and European borrowers.

VICTIMS OF THEIR OWN FOLLY?

Bank critics argue the debt situation is in good part the world's banks own making. They should be held responsible for their own mistakes. It is they and not Mexico, Brazil, Argentina, or other third world debtors that have brought this crisis to a head. It is the banks that have foolishly pumped dollars into these countries.

Thus it is, for instance, that over half of Mexico's debt occurred between 1979-82, an irresponsibly rapid inflow of money into a country whose soaring inflation showed it had far too large a money supply already. Worse, the banks took money from oil-rich depositors and congratulated themselves by lending it to an emerging oil exporter. This was the equivalent of a banking chain-letter. When the price of oil fell, both the deposits and the borrower's capacity to repay were bound to dry up together.

Indeed many bank critics point to additional evidence as proof that bankers made irresponsible credit decisions overseas, thereby contributing to the international debt crisis. Flaws in the banks' loan-evaluation system, including overdependence on one person, ignorance of political factors, and a tendency to make decisions that are more form than substance are among the more specific charges made by critics.

The biggest flaw, according to some critics, is the dominance of line officers in final credit decisions. The line people are the "chiefs" while such support staff people as economists are simply spear bearers with little influence on loan decisions.[8] In short, people who make money are more influential than those who cost money. Indeed, the people who made money achieved their status in the 1970s by doing just that — making money; their reputations were based on selling as much credit as they could. In any staff-line argument the line people prevailed.

There is also the issue of dual allegiance peculiar to international banking. For instance, U.S. banks have tended to hire local citizens to run their foreign offices. The local citizen not only works for an American bank but he is also a citizen of another country. If his or her duty as a representative of an American bank is to exercise caution, his duty to his own country is to lend as much as possible.

Failure to look closely at political factors is another charge directed at bankers. After all, politics can effect a country's ability to repay its debt. Moreover, decisions regarding loan exposure are largely based on recommendations from country credit managers in the field who may misread political factors. To be sure, many banks do have an elaborate system of headquarters checks and balances. Many others also are looking more closely into the sources of their political advice.

A REGULATORY BACKLASH

The banking industry is likely to pay a price for the part some banks have played in promoting loans abroad and then in pushing for increased IMF quotas perceived by many people as a means for bank "bailouts". For instance the American Congress is working on legislation which would, among other things, restrict bank lending abroad. This would be most unfortunate for reasons already noted in this study.

Properly done it can serve to promote development while at the same time be profitable to banks. No doubt many loans were made to developing countries in a large part out of belief that the IMF would bail out the banks if difficulties arose. This problem does need to be addressed, but rushing to add permanent quotas to the IMF may not be the most productive and prudent approach. Indeed our cooperative strategy suggests increasing central control may not be necessary for a successful outcome.

In the United States regulatory agencies are forcing banks to disclose more details about their practices, particularly their troubled loans. At the same time some of those agencies are sweeping aside the protection American banks have against punishment for making those troubled loans: the de facto extension of the 100 percent federal deposit insurance. In effect, such insurance protection will no longer be automatically extended to big depositors (those over $100,000). They will be asked to assume risks hitherto insured by the full faith and protection of the government.

The aim apparently is that if the government can no longer be counted on to insure bank liabilities, it will be necessary for investors to start making judgments on the soundness of individual banks. Investors will want and need to know just what a bank has in its portfolio. There is an obvious difference between an uncollateralized loan to the Mexican or Brazilian government and a fully collateralized one to expand a Florida tourist facility.

As indicated in Table 2.3 a number of other industrial countries also provide deposit insurance. From the view of international banking, however, deposit insurance does not serve a major role in generating the confidence of depositors. The evidence in Table 2.3 suggests that the focus of deposit insurance differs from country to country. It does, however, play an important role in the United States with its large network of small and independent banks.

What is of particular concern in the United States is that banks and thrift institutions since late 1982, by promoting their privileged Federal Deposit Insurance, have lured billions of dollars from money market funds without paying higher returns. Indeed, recent attempts by various concerns such as Sears to buy banks or savings and loans underscore the belief that private institutions with Federal Deposit Insurance can raise money at lower cost than those without it. Such acquisitions, moreover, are reinforced by the practice of electronic banking and by the belief that further deregulation will permit interstate banking and ease current restrictions on the placement of automatic tellers. In sum, many nonbank, nonthrift institutions are attempting to acquire some institutions, no matter how small, that already possess Federal Deposit Insurance for reasons that are not always in tune with traditional American banking. This is another illustration of the changing anatomy of banking which we discussed elsewhere.

Increased disclosure will likely eliminate standard bank secrecy and accounting procedures which have conspired to produce balance sheets inaccessible to many investors. Assets which look very good when carried at book value could at market value be worth significantly less. For instance when the SEC in 1982 began requiring disclosure on foreign loans held by bank holding companies the result raised many an eyebrow. Thus, a few of America's largest banks have almost 170 percent of their shareholders' equity in "troubled" countries, mostly in Latin America. Similar surprises are expected when domestic loans come under closer scrutiny.

Increased disclosure of bank foreign exposure, for instance, would also provide additional information to bank creditors and regulators. An incentive would be provided to spread foreign exposure of banks more broadly and thus reduce heavy country exposures of small banks. This would facilitate a secondary market for foreign loans.

It would also reduce the chances of any single heavily indebted country using the threat debt repudiation so-called "guileful default" as a bargaining method for extracting additional loans on more attractive terms.[9] Threat of debt repudiation is particularly effective in international banking since a bank's methods for dealing with it, including the attachment of a borrowers' assets, are limited particularly when dealing with a foreign government.

There are, of course, other standards by which to measure risks. Banks point, for instance, to liquidity and earnings as appropriate

TABLE 2.3
Bank Deposit Insurance Schemes in Selected Industrial Countries

Country[1]	Date of Establishment	Organizational Status[2]	Funding[3]	Nonbank Deposits Covered[4]	Limits of Coverage per Depositor	Membership Required
Belgium	...[5]	Joint	Pool	All[6,7]	Variable, case by case	Yes
Canada	1967	Official	Pool	All domestic currency[8]	Can$20,000	Yes
France	1979	Private	Unfunded	All domestic currency	F 200,000	Yes
Germany, Fed. Rep. of	1976	Private	Pool	All[7,9]	30% of bank's stated equity capital	No
Italy	—	—	—	—	—	—
Japan	1971	Joint	Small pool	All domestic currency[6,9]	¥ 3,000,000	Yes
Luxembourg	—	—	—	—	—	—
Netherlands	1979	Joint	Unfunded	All but company deposits	f. 30,000	No
Switzerland	Under consideration	...	Pool	All	100% up to Sw F 20,000 75% Sw F 20,000-30,000 50% Sw F 50,000-75,000	Yes[10]
United Kingdom	1982	Official	Small pool	All domestic currency	75% up to £10,000	Yes[10]

| United States | 1933 | Official | Pool | All | US$100,000 | No[11] |

[1] Countries listed are the industrial countries whose banks are active in the international capital markets.

[2] Schemes organized by banks in most cases were undertaken at the initiative of the authorities.

[3] Unfunded schemes are supported by guarantees from the participating banks. Pools often include similar protection. In the United States, for example, the Federal Deposit Insurance Corporation has a credit line with the Treasury.

[4] Liabilities to other banks are usually not covered. Coverage is usually limited to banking entities located within the country. In some cases certain types of deposit are not covered (e.g. *bons de caisse* in France, certificates of deposit in the United Kingdom).

[5] No formal system in effect, but the Rediscount and Guarantee Institute provides financial support to troubled banks, with further support available since 1975 from a supplementary special intervention reserve.

[6] Excludes domestic branches of foreign banks.

[7] Payoff discretionary.

[8] Also covers interbank deposits.

[9] Includes foreign branches of domestic banks.

[10] Except for foreign branches with equivalent coverage from home country.

[11] However, U.S. branches of foreign banks doing retail business and, by state law banks in all but three states must be members.

Source: G. F. Johnson and Richard K. Abrams, *Aspects of the International Banking Safety Net*, Occasional Paper, 17 (Washington: International Monetary Fund, March 1983), p. 21; and Richard Dale, *Bank Supervision Around the World* (New York: Group of Thirty, 1982).

measures. Under the changing regulatory environment, investors are more likely to choose bank capital as the candidate affording them the most protection. In its most general form capital equals net worth (which results when total liabilities are subtracted from total assets). Net worth is owner's equity and can include common preferred, treasury and surplus stock, reserves, and retained earnings. When subordinated notes and debentures are added to the net worth figure the result is "total capital".

Typically bank capital is considered as serving a two-fold function. The first is its function as a cushion against sudden earning loss. Thus without capital to absorb that loss, banks might go bankrupt. For example, if a bank with an equity equal to 10 percent of its assets loses 10 percent of those assets, the entire sum could be absorbed by its capital accounts. Capital offsets portfolio risks and the uninsured depositors would not be affected.

In its second function capital can cushion uninsured depositors and other creditors against loss arising from actual bankruptcy. Consider a liquidation. If after liquidating the bank's assets and paying the insured depositors there is money left, it goes to the general creditors. Holders of equity capital have no claim at all. In sum, the more equity capital, the more the uninsured are insured against losses. In effect, capital offsets bankruptcy risk in this case.

The use of bank capital to judge risk may not be very agreeable to banks. A look at the ratio of equity capital to assets over the past decade indicates that this ratio has been declining and, according to some critics, at a dangerous rate.

This suggests that banks have three options or some combination before them as a consequence of the changing regulatory environment. One is to increase their equity, for example, issue more stock, retain more earnings, increase loan-loss reserves, or take on more long-term debt. This is likely to be expensive. In 1982, for instance, the American banking industry substantially increased loan-loss provisions; however, since additions to loan-loss reserves appear as operating expenses, they reduced reported earnings and dampened profits.

The second option could involve buying private insurance to cover liabilities. This also would be expensive. At the same time it would leave bank portfolios open to judgment by the insurance industry. On the other hand, it would also open the bank to the scrutiny of the market. There is certainly credit to such a proposal.

The third option is to do nothing on capital size and government insurance coverage. This would mean putting bank portfolios and their practices on the line and letting the market assess the risks. If the market disagrees with the judgment of bankers it could prove to be very expensive for banks.

Changing capital requirements will very likely have the most significant impact on very large banks that engage heavily in foreign lending. Their level of capital compared with loan volume, is generally lower than that of small banks. The aim of congressional legislation is in fact directed at increasing bank capital. Considerable flexibility is required nevertheless, if banks are not to be driven away from the international area. That would only make the world debt problems worse and certainly be counterproductive in terms of promoting cooperation.

INTERDEPENDENCE OF WORLD BANKING PROBLEMS

Another important ingredient of our theory of cooperation is that cooperation strategy arrive in such a cluster so as to provide a nontrivial proportion of the interaction each bank has in issues cast up by the international debt problem. The cooperation strategy is all the more important in the real world since capital markets are so well integrated.

Serious problems remain outstanding that must be addressed by the world banking community, their governments, and their clients. For instance, the international flow of capital has become a political issue of prime importance. As a result it is suggested that there is a need for meetings between the large commercial bankers and the semipolitical central bankers of the Bank for International Settlement (BIS). Such an arrangement may in fact not be possible if, as the American Treasury has suggested, banks should turn to their governments for regular advice on countries that merit loans.

Bankers should share information more readily than they have in the past. For instance, there are obvious benefits of a shared information center to monitor how much country X has borrowed up to yesterday rather than as up to six months ago.

Central bankers agreed in the mid 1970s that the regulator of the parent bank should monitor consolidated figures on all that bank's foreign subsidiaries. Italy is not even at the first step. Even the better organized Germans with a law forbidding banks to lend more than three times their capital to any five customers has a significant loophole. Any 99 percent owned off-line subsidiary can still lend what it likes and not report it back.

Since few international banks have collapsed in recent years we do not in fact know how national lenders of last resort will respond to such failures. There are thus far four important examples in the Franklin National Bank in the United States, the Bankhaus I. D. Herstatt, the Israel-British Bank (Israel-Great Britain), and Banco Ambrosiano, Italy. In the Franklin National Bank affair the Federal Reserve accepted responsibility and permitted discount window borrowings to support the bank's branch in London from the time problems were announced until the bank was merged and responsibility for its foreign branches accepted. In all of this the Federal Reserve received cooperative support from the Bank of England.

In the instance of the failure of the Bankhaus I. D. Herstatt, Germany accepted responsibility though the treatment of foreign creditors was an issue for a time. In the end the foreign creditors were treated about as well as domestic creditors underscoring the sensitivity of lenders of last resort to international aspects of bank failures.

In the instance of the Israel-British Bank, matters were more complicated. Both the British and Israeli authorities denied any responsibility, though a compromise of sorts was worked out in the end. Israeli authorities accepted responsibility and the Bank of England contributed, as a compromise, £3 million to the Israel-British Bank's pool of assets.[10]

Less satisfactory is the case of the Italian Banco Ambrosiano which failed in 1982 and was closed and reorganized by Italian authorities. Depositors received full protection. Its 65 percent controlled subsidiary Banco-Ambrosiano Holding of Luxembourg, however, was allowed to fail with no guarantee of depositor protection. Luxembourg authorities and creditors of the Banco-Ambrosiano Holding objected to such treatment of depositors. The authorities in Luxembourg argued that they have no supervisory authority for holding companies, implying that they could not share in lender of last resort responsibilities. The Italian authorities, on the other hand, cited the holding nature of the company. It was not a bank and thus not their responsibility.

Accounting procedures have been inadequate to forewarn investors of coming troubles. The most serious is the manner in which banks' rescheduled country loans are treated. The Polish, Mexican, and Brazilian debts are examples. There are others. Nervousness on the part of bankers that they may have to write these debts off, has prompted some bankers to plead for a "new investor of last resort" to inject new capital into banks. Others feel that it is better to work on a system that allows banks which deserve to go down to do so without taking everyone down with them.

Finally, it is no coincidence that some of the American banks which now find themselves in difficulty have felt frustrated by restrictive legislation that confines them to slower growing parts of the country. To keep expanding they have had to find risky ways around the laws that confine them severely. A case in point is Continental Illinois restricted to a single domestic branch in Chicago.

Frustration of American bankers over their confinement increased thanks to inflation and the resulting high interest rates which promoted financial innovation and collapsed much of the scaffolding supporting bank regulation. Efforts to control banking within the regulatory philosophy of the crisis years of the 1930s has reduced genuine competition and damaged the ability of banks to compete with other financial institutions. Bank price rigging has not worked precisely because banks do face both domestic and foreign competition. Efforts to deal with the situation by denying that it existed were bound to fail.

It is now clear that one must analyze bank loans, money, interest rates, inflation, and exchange rates in the context of globally integrated capital and money markets. No longer is it adequate to view American banking nor that of any other major industrial country as a strictly domestic business to be regulated accordingly.

NOTES

1. *The Christian Science Monitor*, December 17, 1982, p. 11.
2. *The Economist* April 30, 1983, pp. 11-13.
3. *The Economist* April 30, 1983, p. 12.
4. Ibid., p. 12.
5. Ibid.
6. Ibid.
7. Ibid., p. 13.

8. See, for instance, Lawrence Rout, "Banks Revise Way of Making Foreign Loans", *Wall Street Journal*, February 18, 1983, p. 31.

9. See also M. G. Grubel, "Risk Uncertainty and Moral Hazard," *Journal of Risk and Insurance*, March, 1971, pp. 99-106; Allen B. Frankel, "The Lender of Last Resort Facility in the Context of Multinational Banking," *Columbia Journal of World Business* Winter, 1975, pp. 120-27; Richard Dale, *Bank Supervision Around the World* (New York: Group of Thirty, 1982).

10. Joan E. Spero, *The Failure of the Franklin National Bank: Challenge to the International Banking System* (New York: Columbia University Press, 1980), pp. 156-57.

3.

LESSONS FROM THE PAST

IMPORTANCE OF A PROPER ENVIRONMENT

Banks do deserve our concern since the world's prosperity is inked into their account books. Sorting their problems and those of the several debtor countries will take years. Few of the measures undertaken to carry out these tasks will provide much solace for the world's bankers. The anatomy of their industry is indeed changing.

Congress considers forcing bankers to increase reserves for potential losses on foreign loans. Bankers argue that country debt restructurings are working well. Academics push for large one-shot write offs on bank loans to developing countries. And still others insist that debtor countries join in a debt moratorium.

The debates seem endless, but they often boil down to one issue: How to create and maintain cooperation and trust in a world of sovereign states? Our earlier discussion of the ecological tournament underscored the importance of a changing environment based on "good" programs or strategies. "Non-nice" strategies may look promising at the start. In the long run the effect is to destroy the very environment upon which the success of such strategies depend.

Our discussion also underscores the importance of minimizing echo effects in an environment of mutual power. It is important to avoid the systematic error of too competitive a strategy as it is to avoid being too pessimistic about the responsiveness of the other side and not forgiving enough. In effect, the practitioners of a non-nice strategy in our ecological tournament actually wound up punishing

41

themselves, the other player simply serving as a mechanism to delay the self-punishment by a few moves. On the domestic level this is sharply illustrated in the American monetary experience in the 19th century and the internal struggle for monetary supremacy between banks and the government. On the international level we have the examples of the French Indemnity of 1871 and the German Reparations of 1919.

Although the lessons of history are seldom unequivocal it is useful, nevertheless, to turn to past experience, however briefly, to underscore the importance and consistency of our theoretical discussion. Though other episodes come readily to mind, three such historical episodes serve to illustrate our discussion. One is the American experience during the turbulent 1830s and the environment of distrust created by the political struggle for monetary supremacy carried on by the government and banks. The period is characterized by the Bank War, Distribution of Surplus Reserve (Deposit Act of 1836), the Specie Circular, and capital flows.

The second is provided by the French Indemnity Payment of 1871 which set on foot non-nice strategies that actually wound up punishing their practitioners in the post-World War I era. The third illustration is the German reparation payments issue during the post-World War I years. This episode considerably disturbed the international scene of the 1920s and 1930s. In good measure the reparation issue so embittered the Germans (as indeed the earlier indemnity payment of 1871 embittered the French) that they became ever more receptive to extremists whose claims and solutions culminated in World War II. This stands in marked contrast to America's "nice" strategy embedded in the Marshall Plan of 1947 and reconstruction of post-World War II Europe. The Soviet Union and its friends declined an invitation to participate embracing instead a non-nice strategy which in good measure has served to punish its practitioners.

Indeed the Marshall Plan can be considered as that rare occasion in history when the victor actually paid an indemnity to the vanquished. The era of cooperation and good feeling so created between the Americans and Europeans has long outlasted the short term gains of a non-nice strategy as practiced by the Soviet Union in the postwar period.

AMERICAN EXPERIENCE IN THE TURBULENT 1830s[1]

In the post Napoleonic period of deflation which began even before England's resumption of specie payments in 1819, the distress and unemployment which ensued called forth a wide range of protest, including Thomas Attwood's advocacy of inconvertible currency as a means of ensuring full employment.[2] Repeated financial crises followed the failure of English private banks as in 1825. The crises and a growing interest in international trade led to increasing popular acceptance of the gold standard and to the monetary theories on which it is based. By the middle of the century the Ricardian orthodoxy was established, and questionings or qualification of it were swept aside as ill-considered heresies. From time to time, an economist would revive the old issues and question the infallibility of the Ricardian doctrines. It was not until the monetary disturbances following World War I that the critics, as well as the exponents, of these doctrines were again given the attention they merited.

Following 1815, London became the leading source of long term capital.[3] Listings on the London Exchange indicate trends in overseas investment. Immediately after the Napoleonic War British foreign investments were made in European issues. In the 1820s bond issues of the newly created South American states were popular. When these went into default London turned toward the United States.

From 1815 to 1830, the only American issues traded extensively in London were three issues of the United States government, stock of the Second Bank of the United States, bond issues of four states and the bond issues of two municipalities. In 1840, however, the London Exchange listed 46 bond issues of 16 states and the stocks or bonds of 25 canals, railroads and banks. The total quantity of British capital investment in the United States in the 1830s is estimated at $174 million and the better part of this amount $108 million, was incurred from 1835 to 1838. These estimates moreover, are considered an understatement of the true situation.

It was the specie or gold standard which served as the most sensitive tie to American international economic relations and which resulted in changes in the domestic money supply. These changes had important effects on the American economy. As a monetary standard the international specie standard dominated the 19th century economic scene. The successful operation of this standard required participating countries to observe certain rules. Essentially these rules are four in number:

1. The country must take steps to fix the specie value of its national currency.
2. There must be a free import and export of specie into and out of each country which makes up the specie standard system.
3. Each country must make arrangements for the domestic supply of its own money such that the supply of that money goes up when there is a persistent inflow of specie into its territory, and such that it goes down when there is a persistent export of specie out of its territory.

These three rules are sufficient to ensure external balance between the countries on a specie standard. But in order to ensure what we shall call internal balance as well, a further rule must be observed:

4. In each country there must be a reasonable price flexibility.

Although a relatively minor part of the trading world, the United States along with other countries participated in the operation of the international specie standard. This required the United States and others, to observe the four rules enumerated above. In accordance with these rules the exchange rate was fixed. To a first approximation the internal price level in the United States was determined by the external price level; it had to be whatever was necessary in relation to the external price level to keep payments including capital flows in balance. This means that there is a special domestic problem to explain only insofar as internal prices move differently from external prices. It does not mean that domestic conditions cannot affect the internal price level. They can insofar as they affect the conditions of external balance. For example, suppose internal monetary expansion threatens suspension. This will promote a capital outflow that will be deflationary, that is, suspension will be avoided only by an internal price level sufficiently low relative to the external price level to create the surplus to finance the capital outflow.

If the country is not a specie standard, the situation is different. Internal monetary changes affect the price level and through it the exchange rate, so the price level is no longer rigidly linked to price levels abroad.

This link with external conditions is important because internal disturbances may be simply a manifestation of a disturbance more fundamental in nature. Consider the period under study. Not only was the United States a substantial importer of capital from 1834-39 but external prices, as judged by a price index for Britain, in Table 3.1 were rising from 1834-36. Both of these conditions required that the internal stock of money in the United States rise. The only question is how. If, for example, banks expand their notes in circulation this is not, under the assumed conditions, the reason the money supply rises; it is only the form that is taken by a rise that would have occurred one way or another. In other words, in

TABLE 3.1
Indexes of Physical Volume of Trade, Prices, Stock of Money, National Income and Velocity in the United States, 1834-45
(Base: 1834-42 average for volume of trade and prices)

Year (1)	Volume of Trade (2)	Prices* (3)	Stock of Money (in millions of dollars) (4)	National Income (in millions of dollars) (5)	Income Velocity (6)
1834	81	90	152	1,117	7.12
1835	83	107	162	1,393	7.34
1836	95	122	218	1,634	7.40
1837	100	113	224	1,161	7.25
1838	100	105	220	1,589	7.06
1839	100	115	230	1,657	7.65
1840	104	86	203	1,440	7.38
1841	111	87	187	1,286	7.13
1842	106	75	175	1,102	6.80
1843	130	70	149	1,108	6.70
1844	134	73	181	1,331	6.78
1845	167	76	202	1,469	6.88

*Eastern prices.

Sources: See George Macesich, "Sources of Monetary Disturbances in the United States, 1834-1845," *Journal of Economic History*, September, 1960, p. 412 for prices. For Stock of Money, National Income and Income Velocity, unpublished working manuscript. For Volume of Trade same as Figure 3.2.

order for internal balance to be consistent with external balance the money supply had to rise. And, of course, conversely for a period of world deflation and/or cessation of capital imports.

Let us turn now to the main internal factors. These factors arose for the most part from the struggle for monetary supremacy between the partisans of the Second Bank of the United States and the federal government. Though the internal disturbances may have been a manifestation of a disturbance more fundamental in nature, they were undoubtedly important sources of short-term monetary uncertainty and in this way affected the links between external and internal prices. As we shall have occasion to note later, the ebb and flow of the struggle for monetary supremacy frequently cast suspicion on the ability of the United States to maintain the specie standard.

a. Early in the period the mint ratio of silver to gold was changed from 15 to 1 to 16 to 1 affecting the supply conditions of gold in the United States.

b. In 1833, the Second Bank of the United States lost its position as a key depository of federal funds.[4] This institution had been founded in 1816, with one of its functions to serve as banker to the federal government. Tax receipts, mainly from tariffs, were paid into the Bank through customs' collectors in the form of notes of other banks. It was the consensus that the subsequent presentation or threat of presentation of these notes by the Second Bank for payment at the banks of issue constituted a continual check on overissue. Its loss of federal depository status thus initially ended its restraining influence over monetary expansion. The federal government, in turn encouraged expansion by the newly selected depository banks.[5]

c. The Deposit Act, or the Distribution of the Surplus Revenue Act passed in June 1836, called for the distribution of about $37 million to the several states on a per capita basis. The distribution was to be made in four equal installments on January 1837, April 1837, July 1837, and October 1837. The first two installments were transferred, the third was made payable in bank notes irrespective of quality, and the fourth was cancelled.

d. On July 11, 1836, the Treasury department issued what is termed the *Specie Circular*, an order that agents for the sale of public lands should take in payment only specie, and should no longer receive the notes issued by banks. The Specie Circular was repealed in May 1838. The expected effect of the Deposit

Act and the Specie Circular is that they ushered in a substantial shift in the "specie ballast" affecting bank reserves and ultimately the money supply. And, in addition, they increased domestic and foreign distrust in the ability of the United States to maintain the specie standard.

e. On May 10, 1837, the banks of New York suspended specie payments, and they were shortly followed by banks in other parts of the country; resumption occurred from May through August 1838. The banks of Philadelphia suspended again on October 9, 1839 and did not resume effectively until March 1842; in this they were followed by others throughout the country. We should expect the initial effect to have been to prevent or postpone a contraction that would otherwise have occurred.

f. During the period of suspension the new state bank depository arrangement for handling government funds was discredited. Following a period of political agitation a new arrangement for handling government funds was made. This arrangement was called the Independent Treasury System. The first use of the Independent Treasury System was short lived. The Act of July 4, 1840, was repealed August 13, 1841. Thereafter and until 1846, bank notes were accepted by the Treasury and deposits of the federal government went to state banks on terms similar to those under which the transfer from the Second Bank had been made in 1833. We should expect that this operation had an expansionary effect on bank reserves and ultimately on the money supply. However, we should not expect the effect to be as pronounced as in the earlier period, since government deposits had become almost negligible.

In conclusion, it is interesting to note that contrary to the views of contemporaries and the views of more recent students, the monetary damage done by the internal struggle for monetary supremacy and its concomitant uncertainty, by making a large specie stock desirable, kept the money supply from rising as much as it otherwise would have rather than that it produced too rapid a rise in the money supply.

Let us turn now to documentation of the movements of money, prices, income, velocity and the physical volume of trade in more detail over the turbulent period 1834-45.

The series on money, prices, income, velocity, and the physical volume of trade are presented in Table 3.1 and in Figures 3.1 and 3.2. Four geographical wholesale price series and three sector wholesale price series are presented in Figure 3.1. Three of the geographical price series are for internal, or domestic, prices in the United States, while the remaining series is for external prices. The three sector price series are for industrial, agricultural, and import prices. The physical volume of trade index is composed of series on selected raw materials, transportation, and foreign trade. They are presented in Figure 3.2.

FIGURE 3.1
Index of Prices. (Annually, 1834-45; Base, 100 = 1834-42 Average; Scale, Semi-Log).

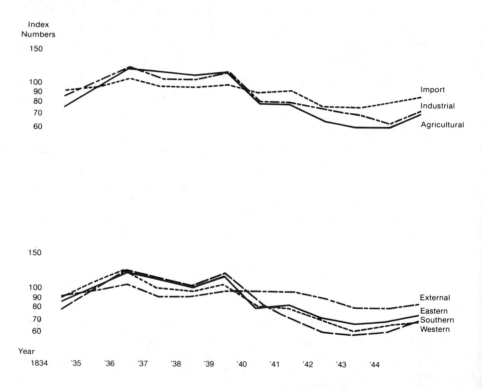

Source: George Macesich, "Sources of Monetary Disturbances in the United States, 1834-1845," *Journal of Economic History* (September, 1960): 411.

FIGURE 3.2
**Index of Physical Volume of Trade and Components of Physical
Volume of Trade.** (Annually, 1834-45; Base, 100 = 1834-42 Average;
Scale, Semi-Log).

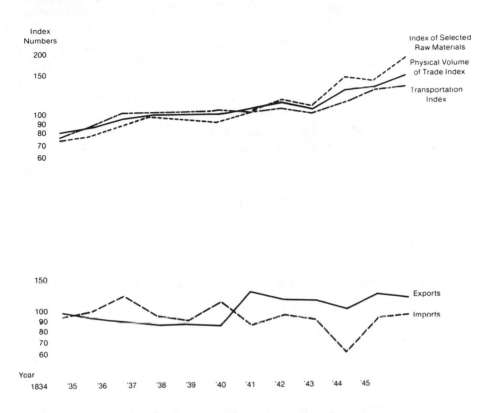

Source: George Macesich, "Physical Volume of Trade Index," Unpublished
working manuscript.

As shown in Figure 3.1 there is an initial decided rise in prices
from 1834 to 1836, then a decline to 1838, then a peak in 1839,
then a sharp decline interrupted by a brief spurt in 1841, then a
decline until 1843, followed by a much slower rise during the final
years.

These periods of divergent price movements are reflected in our
other series and thus divide the period 1834-45 into five reasonably
well defined segments: (1) the initial rise from 1834 to 1836. This

segment was characterized by an extraordinarily rapid rise in the stock of money, national income, and in the physical volume of trade which increased but at drastically reduced rates; (2) the period 1836 to 1838. This was a short but sharp contraction during which the stock of money and internal prices declined while external prices increased from 1837 to 1838; (3) the period 1838 to 1839. This segment is characterized by rapid rise in the stock of money, national income, internal prices, external prices, and no change in the physical volume of trade; (4) the contraction from 1839 to 1843. This was an unusually sharp contraction during which the stock of money, national income, internal prices, and external prices, interrupted by a brief spurt in 1841, declined sharply, internal prices fell sharply relative to external prices, and the physical volume of trade remained comparatively stable; (5) the expansion from 1843 to 1845. This segment is characterized by a rise in the money stock, national income in internal and external prices, and in physical volume of trade.

In very broad terms, at this point, the explanation during these periods is reasonably clear:

1. 1834-1836. The initial rapid expansion reflected a combination of favorable internal and external factors. On the internal side, the sharp contraction in 1833-34, during the so-called "Bank War," was brief but severe; once it was over, there tended to be a vigorous rebound. On the external side, worldwide expansion coupled with heavy capital inflows permitted an internal price rise without external difficulties.

2. 1836-1838. The subsequent contraction had its source in a combination of two factors. In the first place, external prices fell from 1836 to 1837. This alone would have required internal prices to decline. In the second place, a combination of government actions cast suspicion on the ability of the United States to maintain the specie standard and a "flight" from the dollar occurred. This would have required the internal prices to decline in order to finance the domestic and foreign flight from the dollar. The required internal price fall resulted in a financial panic in mid 1837. The panic led to a suspension of specie payments. The exchange rate depreciated and internal prices increased. Internal prices declined in late 1837 and in early 1838 and resumption of specie payments occurred in mid-1838.

3. 1838-1839. The second expansion reflected a combination of favorable internal and external factors. On the internal side, the resumption of specie payments coupled with the repeal of the Specie Circular discouraged flight from the dollar. This relieved the pressure on internal prices. On the external side, external prices increased from 1837 to 1839. This permitted an internal price rise without external difficulties.
4. 1839-1843. The subsequent sharp contraction reflected primarily an unfavorable set of external factors. External prices declined from 1839 to 1843. The required internal price fall was further intensified by the cessation of the heavy capital inflow of earlier years and by some repatriation of foreign investment. The sharp decline in internal prices was the only alternative if the specie standard was to be maintained by the United States.
5. 1843-1845. The level of internal prices reached by the United States by 1843 was lower relative to external prices. The year 1843 is characterized by a heavy specie inflow. The specie inflow temporarily filled the gap in payments that would otherwise have required either an appreciation of the dollar relative to other currencies — ruled out by the fixed exchange rate under the specie standard — or a more rapid rise in internal United States prices. At the same time, the large specie inflow provided the basis and stimulus for an expansion in the money stock and prices from 1844 to 1845. The expansion of the money stock and prices led to a reduction in the specie inflow in 1844 and to an outflow in 1845.

FRENCH INDEMNITY PAYMENT OF 1871

If the issue over monetary supremacy in our American example is one of non-nice domestic strategies, the French Indemnity arose as a consequence of the Franco-Prussian War and the struggle for political supremacy in Europe between France and Prussia. Their instruments of policy were indeed non-nice strategies. The resultant poisoned atmosphere had wide-ranging consequences for both countries as well as the rest of the world.

It is thus useful to present briefly the background of the Franco-Prussian War of 1870-71. The collapse of the revolutionary movement in Europe in 1849 was a great disappointment to the liberals of Germany. Little progress had been made toward the establishment of a representative government and Germany still remained split into some three dozen states, the rulers of which clung ferociously to their independent sovereignty. Within two decades, however, a large measure of unity was to be achieved.

The driving force needed for this accomplishment came from Prussia. King Wilhelm I of Prussia succeeded to the throne in 1861. The new king, who was in his mid-60s, had little love for liberal institutions. At his coronation he crowned himself with the words, "I receive this crown from the hands of God." His one enthusiasm was for the army. He was convinced that Prussia could reassert its claims to leadership in Germany only if it had a large army to support these claims. Like Frederick the Great he believed that diplomacy without arms is music without instruments. To assist him in this task he chose as minister of war General von Roon (1803-1879), one of the great military organizers of the nineteenth century, and as chief of the general staff, General von Moltke (1800-1891).

In order to overcome the resistance of the Prussian Chamber of Deputies or lower house for a large army, General von Roon brought in Otto von Bismarck in whom he had confidence. Appointed minister-president on September 21, 1862, Bismarck remained in power for the next 28 years. On September 30, 1862 he sounded the keynote to future Prussian policy in an address to the finance committee of the lower house. "Germany," he declared, "looks not to liberalism of Prussia, but to its power. . . . The great questions of the time cannot be solved by speeches and parliamentary majorities — that was the mistake of 1848 and 1849 — but by blood and iron." When the lower house still refused to vote a huge army budget Bismarck simply went out and collected the taxes on his own. He was, as he wrote, "the most vigorously and best hated person in the country."[6]

Bismarck's manipulation of Austria, Russia, and France are good illustrations of the short-term success of non-nice strategies. His cultivation of Russia and France for the purpose of isolating Austria against whom he had aggressive designs are well known. He offered Russia help in 1863 to put down the Polish insurrection. He tricked Napoleon III of France into remaining neutral in the event of an Austro-Russian War by dropping hints in 1865 of possible compensations to France in the event of a Russian victory over Austria.

His manipulation of the Schleswig-Holstein question which ultimately provided the pretext for war with Austria made it appear as if Prussia were being forced into hostilities and demonstrated what some consider as "great diplomatic skill. . . . Like a magician he permitted his opponents and the Prussian public to see only the cards he wanted them to see. While he was publicly feigning willingness to submit the question to arbitration, under cover he manipulated the factors in such a way as to foredoom any attempt to arbitration. At all times he was careful to give the impression that Austria refused to be conciliated. Deftly he shifted from argument to argument until the preparations for war were complete and the struggle could begin. He himself was proud of his work. In later years he said "Schleswig-Holstein, that is the campaign, politically speaking, of which I am the proudest."[7]

The Austro-Prussian War, also known as the Seven Weeks' War, began in June 1866 and ended in July of the same year. In the terms of peace which he offered Austria Bismarck showed that he was not adverse to a nice strategy, "Having wrested the Germany bureaucracy from Austria," he was careful not to make his demands so severe that they would stir a desire for vengeance. He wished to secure Austria for an ally. Hence despite the clamors of the military party, he stood firm in his refusal to annex any Austrian territory, thereby rendering possible a speedy reconciliation of the belligerents. By the terms of the treaty of peace signed at Prague in August, 1866, Austria was compelled only to pay a small indemnity and to transfer her rights in Schleswig-Holstein to Prussia. She had to consent, however, to the dissolution of the Germanic Confederation and the foundation of a new organization of Germany without the participation of the empire of Austria. "Thus was Austria excluded from all participation in German politics."[8]

With Austria out of the way, it was France's turn. The principal goal of Bismarck's striving was to bring on war with France the aggressor. The pretext was soon provided over the question of the Hohenzollern candidature for the Spanish throne. German Prince Leopold's acceptance in 1870 moved the French to demand a withdrawal from King Wilhelm I. This the king refused to do only to have Leopold refuse to accept the crown. The matter seemed settled when the French empress and foreign minister insisted on a promise from the Prussian king that he would at no future time consent to have a member of the Hohenzollern family become a candidate for the

Spanish throne. King Wilhelm I refused to give any such assurances. The French ambassador insisted on yet another interview, he was told that the matter would have to be taken up with the King's ministers. Up to that point the exchange of views had not been offensive.

When the King informed Bismarck by telegram of what had taken place "Bismarck took a pencil and began to edit the telegram. When he had finished his version, which he hoped would have the effect of a red flag upon the Gallic bull, he sent it to be published in an extra evening edition of the official newspaper. The result was exactly what he desired. While on the one hand, it left with the German people the impression that the French ambassador had been insolent, on the other it led the French to believe that their ambassador had been insulted. Indignation flared up in both countries. In Paris the populace as well as the ministers and deputies clamored for war so loudly that the advocates of peace could not be heard. Only Napoleon III still hesitated. Finally he, too, gave way and war was formally declared on July 19, 1870."[9]

Bismarck had gotten his war with France as the apparent aggressor thanks to the now infamous Ems telegram. The war ended disastrously for France. It was ended by the almost equally disastrous Treaty of Frankfurt, in May 1871. Under its terms France was required to pay an indemnity of 5 billion gold francs, considered a very large sum indeed for the period. France also lost Alsace, including Strasbourg, and part of Lorraine, including Metz, to the new German Empire. France refused to be reconciled to the loss of these territories. Even Bismarck thought the territorial settlement unwise. His plan was to annex Alsace which was largely German, but finally permitted himself to be overruled by the military party.

In addition to the humiliating Treaty of Frankfurt, France suffered an earlier humiliation of having King Wilhelm proclaimed emperor in the Hall of Mirrors at Versailles. Thus, Bismarck's non-nice strategy of "blood and iron" worked — albeit in the short-run. All Germany except the German provinces of Austria was united under the bureaucracy of Prussia. In the long term, however, the strategy was self-defeating. It squeezed out and eliminated from the tournament the very ones upon whose existence the success of such a strategy depended. The full bill for all of this was to be paid two generations later by the Germans as well as others.

As for the war indemnity itself, the Treaty of Frankfurt provided that more than 5 billion francs be transferred in a few large sums by March 2, 1874. To the surprise of many the amount was transferred quickly. In fact, the final installment was paid on September 15, 1873. Moreover, comparatively little disturbance was observed in economic activity in Europe as a result of the rapid transfer of so large a sum.

The actual amount of the transfer as provided by the Treaty was about 5.3 billion francs.[10] Deducted from this amount was 325 million francs for railroads in Alsace-Lorraine belonging to the Chemin de Fer de l'Est, whose shareholders were to be compensated by the French government. Banque of France notes were accepted for an amount of 125 million francs. Transferred in gold or in foreign bills was the remainder of the 4,865 million francs. No payments in kind were made.

Of the 4,865 million francs only a small amount was transferred in cash. Haberler provides us with the following breakdown:

1.	In German coin, which for the most part was brought into France by German troops and by the French Government	105 million francs
2.	In gold buillion	273 million francs
3.	In silver	617 million francs
4.	In bills of exchange	4,148 million francs
		4,865 million francs

These amounts were raised by France through large scale liquidation of capital in French banks and borrowing. Thanks to two conditions, the loans of 1871 and 1872 were relatively easy for France to negotiate. First, in spite of the war defeat, the country's national credit remained good. Secondly, France had sizable foreign investment by 1870. From the middle of the 19th century on France was a typical creditor country, investing much of her savings abroad and living to a considerable extent on the interest and dividends. The country's balance of payments remained passive for years owing to annual receipts from foreign investments which exceeded annual exports of capital.

The success with which France mobilized these foreign investments is indicated by the fact that in 1871 and 1872 two large loans were issued amounting to 5,792 million francs. Indeed, the second loan was so successful that it was ten-fold oversubscribed. Again Haberler provides us with the sources of these loans:[11]

1. About 2,250 million francs were subscribed from abroad — indeed a sizable amount from Germany.
2. About 2,200 million francs were taken by French nationals who liquidated their foreign holdings for this purpose. This meant, in effect, a substantial transfer of capital. The French Government in effect indirectly borrowed the foreign investments in private hands, thus obtaining the francs necessary to buy foreign bills. In some instances the Government accepted payment for its stock directly in foreign script which it could then sell abroad.
3. The source of the balance 1,500 million francs is uncertain but is presumed to have come out of the country's current savings.

In effect, the bulk of the indemnity was raised by borrowing. To be sure the amount of the indemnity had to be reflected in France's reduced consumption. The burden to the French taxpayer, however, was spread over many years. The annual interest service on the new debt amounted to about 374.6 million francs. Although paid off rapidly and the interest rate reduced by conversions, the burden of the indemnity on the French treasury went beyond World War I.

The effect of the indemnity on France's international trade is suggested in Table 3.2. Except for the years 1872-1875, the country's balance of trade was passive. The outflow of goods began shortly after the first transfer of capital and this continued for several years. This was eased by 1876 when a passive balance was registered. Indeed, it is interesting that direct-commodity exports from France to Germany which registered an average of only 260 million francs in 1868-69 rose to 436 million francs in 1872-73. Although transfer is normally made in commodities and services, only a part of these are transferred direct from the country making payments to the country receiving them.

In fact fewer goods and services were exported from France than expected. The reason for this is that Germany used part of the money to introduce the gold standard in the country and thus did not spend on imports. About 750 million francs were spent by Germany on introducing the gold standard which otherwise would have required an increase in loans and/or taxes. Another 120 million

TABLE 3.2
France's Balance of Trade, 1867-78
(in millions of francs)

Year	Imports	Exports	Surplus
1867	3,202	3,085	−117
1868	3,415	2,974	−441
1869	3,269	3,257	−12
1870	2,935	2,915	−20
1871	3,599	2,925	−674
1872	3,603	3,814	+211
1873	3,651	3,925	+274
1874	3,574	3,806	+232
1875	3,585	3,968	+383
1876	4,046	3,689	357
1877	3,737	3,552	−185
1878	4,246	3,297	−949

Source: Gottfried Haberler, *The Theory of International Trade* (London: William Hodge & Co., 1950), p. 95.

francs was deposited in gold in the Fortress of Spandau. An undetermined sum was spent by the German treasury on pensions, repayment of debt, and on military facilities.

Unfortunately, we do not have adequate data to trace through the economics of all the various implications of the indemnity. For instance, it would be useful to see the effects of the payments on Germany and if in fact they helped to produce the economic boom which subsequently led up to the crisis in 1873.

THE POST-WORLD WAR I GERMAN REPARATIONS AND DEBT EPISODE[12]

At the Paris Peace Conference peacemakers of World War I were much absorbed by the questions of reparations, which in some respects was the storm center of the peace conference. Germany was believed to be solely responsible for the war by almost everyone present. This belief was endorsed by Americans as well as Europeans. The conviction caused the peacemakers to include in the treaty the so-called "war-guilt clause." According to it (Article 231): "Germany accepts the responsibility of Germany and her Allies for causing all the loss and damage to which the Allied and Associated Governments and their nationals have been subjected, as a consequence of the war imposed upon them by the aggression of Germany and her Allies." Since Germany was the guilty author of the war, it followed logically that she and her allies should pay the entire cost of the war. This did not satisfy many in France including the French press which demanded in addition the repayment with interest of the indemnity Germany had collected from France in 1871.

After much debate, it was finally decided to submit the entire question of reparation to a special commission which was to determine by May 1, 1921, both the amount and manner of payment. As a first payment Germany was required to pay at once the sum of $5 billion in the form of gold, merchant ships, reconstruction material, coal, dyestuffs, and other commodities.[13] In June 1920 the Allies reached an agreement on the sum total of reparations. The agreement was revised in January 1921 in that Germany was to pay 226 billion gold marks in 42 annual installments rising gradually to 6 billion marks per year, 12 percent of the annual value of German exports, the costs of the Allied military occupation, and various commissions.[14]

A German counter-offer of 50 billion gold marks less 20 billion marks already transferred was rejected. The allies then applied sanctions occupying several German cities, placing a tariff on German imports and creating a custom barrier in the Rhineland between the occupied area and the rest of Germany.

Matters improved and in London in May 1921 the sum total of German Reparations was fixed at 132 billion gold marks or about $32 billion. This sum served as the basis for the terms incorporated into the agreement reached in May, 1921. Accordingly the reparations sum was fixed at 132 billion gold marks less the amounts already paid; responsibility for the debt of about 6.6 billion marks which Belgium contracted during the war with her allies; the entire amount to be paid in annual installments of 2 billion marks plus 26 percent of the value of German imports beginning on May 1, 1921; and 1 billion marks was to be transferred within a month.

It soon became evident that the May 1921 London agreement was unworkable. Germany was simply unable to raise the necessary volume of foreign bills. Application was made in December, 1921 for a moratorium and in January, 1922 the annual payments were reduced provisionally to 1,450 million gold marks in kind and 720 million in cash. By 1922 it became equally clear that Germany could not carry out the provisions and applied for a new moratorium and thereafter continued to press for revision of payments.

In the meantime France, in order to secure payments in kind, had devised a sort of mortgage scheme not only on Germany's revenue but also its industrial firms and organizations. Failure to make deliveries in kind served as a pretext for France and Belgium to occupy the Ruhr in 1923. Thereupon Germany suspended all reparation payments to France and Belgium and attempted passive resistance. By the autumn of 1923 such resistance was futile and Germany redoubled its efforts to scale down reparation payments.

By 1923 the German mark collapsed. A special committee of the Reparations Commission headed by General Dawes, an American, drew up recommendations that served as a first step toward revision of the London Agreement of 1921. Known as the Dawes Plan the idea was to improve Germany's paying capacity by rehabilitating her economy and finances. To enable Germany to return to the gold standard a $200 million loan was arranged mainly subscribed by the United States. In effect, the amount was about four-fifths of the reparations installment payable during the first year of the Dawes Plan. There was to be a two year moratorium in the interests of German economic recovery. Thereafter reparations were to be paid on annuities, using in 1929-30 2.5 billion marks, or about $600 million, and remaining thereafter at that amount. There were also to be supplementary annuities varying in accordance with a complex index of German prosperity. Of the 2.5 billion marks 960 million were to be paid annually for 30-some years, while annuities consisting of the remaining 1,540 million were to be continued indefinitely. In effect, Germany was to pay tribute forever. Furthermore, a "gold clause" provided that nominal amounts to be paid would vary with changes in the purchasing power of gold.

A reparations agent was to receive the annuities and transfer them to governments receiving reparations. He was charged with actually changing the marks into foreign money. If the German exchange rate threatened to depreciate he was to suspend transfer. In that event the sums paid over should accumulate up to 5 billion marks with additional contributions being reduced in amount.

The 960 million marks in fixed annuities were to be raised not by the German treasury but by the country's railways and industry. The railways were responsible for a total of 11 billion marks and industry for 5 billion marks. The idea, apparently, was to commercialize this amount of the reparations payment through the creation of marketable securities.

The German central bank or *Reichbank* was placed under international control and its independence from the German government assured by international law. A board of 14 directors (some Germans and some foreigners) were to examine the Bank reports and a foreign commissioner was to see to note issue and reserves of the Bank. This was to make impossible any attempts to use inflation as a means for escaping payment of reparations.

The Dawes Plan seemed to operate well even though it was considered only a provisional agreement. It did not fix the amount of reparations nor the number of annuities. It was really aimed at gauging Germany's ability to pay. On this score it missed. What was demonstrated was that during the four years under the Dawes Plan the sum envisioned could be transferred without too much trouble. Since these payments were paid out of the large foreign loans raised by Germany, not much was demonstrated about the country's capacity to pay. By the end of 1928 it became clear that something more permanent had to be done to resolve the reparations issue.

In 1929 another international committee under the chairmanship of Owen Young drew up the Young Plan. In the Hague conferences of August 1929 and January 1930 the Young Plan was elaborated and discussed at length. For agreeing to a final settlement Germany received a further scaling-down of payments, withdrawal of Allied troops, and an end to the control of her finances. There were to be reparations payments amounting to 1,989 million marks (about $28 billion) in 59 annual payments coming to an end in 1988. Belgium was to receive 9.3 and 26 million marks annually until 1966 on account of paper marks issued during the German occupation. There were to be annuities representing the cost of the American Army of Occupation and claims to compensation by American nationals. A sum of 600 million marks of the Young annuities were to be transferred unconditionally. Germany, however, could apply to the newly established organization to handle reparations (the Bank International Payments) for a transfer moratorium. The assent of the creditors was not required. A committee of the Bank would then examine the situation and make its recommendation for revision. Part of the German obligation could be commercialized by the issue of interest-bearing bonds, which claiming countries could sell at once. The gold clauses and the "index of prosperity" were abolished along with international boards including the Reparations Commission itself. The German treasury assumed the burden of the reparations and private industry was free from all liability, and bonds already issued including those of railways were cancelled. There was, however, a special reparations tax of 600 million marks placed on the railways.

Within two years it became clear that the Young Plan was unworkable. The worldwide depression beginning in 1929 was particularly severe in Germany. By the summer of 1931 it was doubtful that any of the Young Plan annuities could be paid. President Hoover put forth a proposal calling for a moratorium on all political war debts. The moratorium from July 1931 to June 1932 kept the Young Plan nominally in force. Shortly after Hoover's call for a moratorium Germany was struck by a banking crisis brought on by the Great Depression. Under the terms of the Young Plan the German government could and did call for the Bank for International Settlements to meet and consider what should be done when the Hoover moratorium expired.

For all practical purposes the war debt payments came to an end together with Germany's reparation payments by the Lausanne Agreement of July 1932. Reparations were reduced to 3 billion marks to be paid by the German government to the Bank for International Settlements in 5 percent redeemable bonds. Germany's other liabilities were all cancelled except the service of the Dawes Loan and the Young Loan of 1930.

Throughout the reparation issue ran the thread of interallied war debts. The United States had become a net creditor for over $10 billion. Great Britain had both borrowed and lent and come out a net creditor of $4.5 billion. France owed over $3.5 billion net. All these amounts are exclusive of interest. The other countries owed smaller amounts. Britain pressed for a cancellation of all war debt at the peace conference in 1919. And indeed in 1922 declared that it would expect no more from its debtors than it had itself to pay to the United States. France argued that the debts should be regarded as contributions made to the common banks.

The Americans did not agree that a legal connection existed between interallied debts and German reparations payments. They saw their loans as strictly commercial enterprises to be paid with interest. Given America's high tariff policy in the 1920s (Fordney-McCumber Tariff, 1922) and again in the 1930s (Smoot-Hawley Tariff), repayment was very difficult indeed. Some money was collected from American debtors thanks to private loans to Germany which made possible some reparations payments and so in turn interallied debts.

According to various estimates Germany paid about 25 billion gold marks from Versailles until the Dawes Plan and about 11 billion under the Dawes and Young Plans totalling about $9 billion. To judge from the estimates of the Reparations Commission, Germany paid about $5 billion. German estimates, however, place the figure at better than $15 billion.[15] It received from abroad about $8.5 billion during this period mostly from loans after 1924. Indeed, after 1924 German borrowings abroad ran almost double the country's reparations payments. As a result the problem of generating a current account surplus large enough to offset the reparations transfers was simply put aside thanks in good part to lack of foreign demand for German goods undoubtedly produced by world tariff policies of the period.

This international financial circus was brought to a sudden end by the Great Depression of 1929 when American loans to Germany ceased. German industry had been reconstructed and strengthened, but democratic government in Germany had been undermined partly by the reparations issue. International relations among wartime Allies as well as between Germany and the Allies had become embittered. In effect, attempts to collect war debts and make reparations payments proved to be one colossal failure. It is an experiment which has important lessons to recommend to contemporaries in search of solutions to the more than $600 billion debt of the world's developing countries.

NOTES

1. This section draws on some of my unpublished and published work on American monetary experience in the 19th century when the United States too was a developing country with large foreign borrowing. See, for example, George

Macesich, "Sources of the Monetary Disturbances in the U.S. 1834-45," *Journal of Economic History*, September, 1960, pp. 407-34.

2. See, for example, D. J. Moss, "Banknotes versus gold: the Monetary Theory of Thomas Attwood in his early writings, 1816-19." *History of Political Economy*, Spring, 1981, pp. 19-38.

3. L. H. Jenks, *The Migrations of British Capital to 1875* (New York and London: A. A. Knopf, 1927), chapters II and III.

4. At no time, however, was the Second Bank a sole depository for the government. At various outlying points, the Treasury and collectors of revenue had no choice but to use state banks. W. B. Smith, *Economic Aspects of the Second Bank of the United States* (Cambridge: Harvard University Press, 1953).

5. *Reports of the Secretary of the Treasury of the United States* (Washington: Blair, 1837), pp. III, 369.

6. Robert Ergong, *Europe Since Waterloo*, 3d ed. (Lexington: D. C. Heath and Company, 1967), pp. 161-62.

7. Ibid., pp. 162-63.

8. Ibid., pp. 164-65.

9. Ibid., pp. 167-68.

10. See Gottfried Haberler, *Theory of International Trade* (London: William Hodge & Co., 1950), p. 93.

11. Ibid., p. 94.

12. From the vast literature on the subject, I draw primarily on the following: Paul Alpert, *Twentieth Century Economic History of Europe* (New York: Henry Schuman, 1951), John H. Clapham, "Europe After the Great Wars, 1816 and 1920," *Economic Journal* (Dec., 1920), pp. 423-35; Theodore E. Gregory, "The Economic Significance of 'Gold, Maldistribution,'" *Manchester School of Economics and Social Studies* II, no. 2 (1931), pp. 77-138; Ibid., *Gold, Unemployment and Capitalism* (London: P. S. King and Son, 1933); Ibid., *The Gold Standard and Its Future*, 3rd ed. (New York: E. P. Dutton & Co., Inc., 1935); Ibid., "Rationalization and Technological Unemployment," *Economic Journal* (Dec., 1930), pp. 441-67; John M. Keynes, "The City of London and the Bank of England, August, 1914," *Quarterly Journal of Economics* (Nov. 1914), pp. 48-71; Ibid., *The Economic Consequences of Mr. Churchill* (London: Hogarth Press, 1925); *The Economic Consequences of the Peace* (London: Macmillan & Co., Ltd., 1920) Ibid., "The Economics of War in Germany," *Economic Journal* (Sept. 1914), pp. 442-52; John M. Keynes, *The End of Laissez-Faire* (London: Hogarth Press, 1927); John M. Keynes, "The French Stabilization Law," *Economic Journal* (Sept. 1928), pp. 490-94; John M. Keynes, "The German Transfer Problem," *Economic Journal* (March, 1929), p. 107; John M. Keynes, *A Revision of the Treaty* (London: Macmillan & Co., Ltd., 1922); John M. Keynes, "War and the Financial System August, 1914," *Economic Journal* (Sept. 1914), pp. 460-86; John M. Keynes with H. D. Henderson, *Can Lloyd George Do It? An Examination of the Liberal Pledge* (London: Nation & Athenaeum, 1919); John M. Keynes, *Essays in Persuasion* (New York: Harcourt, Brace and Company, 1932). James W. Angell, "Reparations," in the *Encyclopedia of Social Sciences* vol. 13 (New York: Macmillan, 1930), pp. 300-08; Gottfried Haberler, *Theory of International Trade* (London: William Hodge

& Co., 1950); W. Arthur Lewis, *Economic Surveys 1919-1939* (London: Allen & Unwin, 1949); Frank D. Graham, *Exchange, Prices, and Production in Hyperinflation: Germany, 1920-1923* (Princeton: Princeton, 1930); Constantine Bresciani-Turron, *The Economics of Hyperinflation* (London: George Allen & Unwin, 1937); Phillip Cagan, "The Monetary Dynamics of Hyperinflation," in Milton Friedman (ed.), *Studies in the Quantity Theory of Money*, pp. 25-117; Leland B. Yeager, *International Monetary Relations: Theory, History and Policy* (New York: Harper & Row, 1966); Milton Friedman and Anna J. Schwartz, *A Monetary History of the U.S., 1867-1960* (Princeton: Princeton University Press, 1963); George Macesich, *The International Monetary Economy and the Third World* (New York: Praeger Publishers, 1981); C. P. Kindleberger, *Manias, Panics, and Crashes: A History of Financial Crises* (New York: Basic Books, 1978).

13. The Paris Peace Conference produced not one treaty, but five. In addition to the treaty of Versailles it drew up the treaty of St. Germain with Austria, the treaty of Sèvres with Turkey, (superseded by the treaty of Lausanne in 1923) the treaty of Trianon with Hungary and the treaty of Neuilly with Bulgaria. Like that of Versailles, each of the others took its name from one of the suburbs of Paris. The treaty of Versailles was the model for the rest, and many of its sections, as for example the Covenant of the League were incorporated in all. Reparations were demanded from Austria, Hungary, and Bulgaria in the same terms as from Germany. Subsequent American repudiation of the Treaty was a severe blow to the entire Versailles settlement. On July 2, 1921 the United States signed a separate treaty with Germany.

14. Gottfried Haberler, *Theory of International Trade* (London: William Hodge & Co., 1950), p. 103.

15. By way of contrast it is interesting to note that between 1946 and 1958 the United States gave military grants of $16.8 billion to West Europe and $6.1 billion to other countries; the first eight years of the Marshall Plan cost the American taxpayers $58 billion; the period of lend-lease assistance from July 1, 1940 to July 1, 1945 cost the American taxpayers a net recouped assistance and payments of about $41 billion. George Macesich, *The International Monetary Economy and the Third World* (New York: Praeger Publishers, 1981), p. 64.

4.

IN SEARCH OF SOLUTIONS

PERSPECTIVE

The debt crisis has accelerated what was already coming: the painful integration of major developing countries into the mainstream of the world economy. This is an opportunity for the world to move up the ratchet of cooperation as our theory of cooperation suggests. World banks can and do serve as instruments (or clusters) for promoting a Tit for Tat strategy of cooperation.

Bankers are correct in lamenting the expedient shortness of some politicians' memories. What causes such concern is the move within Congress to restrict their international lending which, in effect, would be contrary to our theory of cooperation. It was only a few years back, they note, that numerous congressmen and certainly many high government officials were praising banks for their ability to recycle petrodollars of the OPEC oil cartel.

A policy of encouraging foreign lending is a correct one and should be continued as a means for developing cooperation and inter-dependence as well as mutual profit. To defect from such a strategy would be very shortsighted indeed. The importance of maintaining and preserving an environment in which a strategy of cooperation will flourish and thrive is underscored in our discussion of lessons from the past. Banks should not have their cluster role in promoting such an environment circumscribed by misdirected if well intended measures. Indeed, they should be encouraged and competitively strengthened to continue this role as we shall discuss in the next chapter.

The IMF and other groups estimate a need for $15 billion to $20 billion in new commercial bank financing — short- and long-term — by the developing countries in 1983 to meet their obligations and speed development. This is about a 7 percent increase over total 1982 exposure according to these sources.

Some argue that the current international strategy for dealing with the developing-country problem is inadequate. This strategy relies on national industrial recovery, lower interest rates, reduced protectionism against developing-country exports, more austerity in these nations to reduce their demand for imports and to increase exports, and levels of capital inflow to the developing countries which are, at best, equal to their debt service payments.

In addition to strengthening the IMF and World Bank, critics argue, creditor banks should be "realistic" in setting terms of reschedulings and provide adequate additional funds. Bankers too will have to consider the issue of whether the increased interest, margins, and front-end fees charged at the time of rescheduling are appropriate to the situation.

There is a question whether the economic recovery from the 1979-83 recession will be strong enough to let the politicians of industrial nations reduce trade barriers. There is also the question whether the debtors can sustain their austerity program politically and socially. It may well be that far more is being demanded of the major debtors by way of adjustment than could be accepted by any of the industrial nations. These measures, moreover, come on top of a situation that has already been deteriorating.

According to Federal Reserve Board data, American banks had medium- and long-term loans to non-OPEC developing countries and Eastern European countries of some $108.2 billion as of June 1982. This money is spread over many countries and many institutions.

The seven biggest developing-country borrowers are Argentina, Brazil, Chile, Mexico, South Korea, the Philippines, and Taiwan. Here the exposure of U.S. banks was $79.5 billion. It is, however, the Latin American borrowers that are the most worrisome to bankers.

Total capital of American banks long-term plus the shareholders' equity, was $66.2 billion in mid-1982. So their loans to non-OPEC developing countries and Eastern Europe were more than 1.6 times their capital. On the one hand regarding this risk question, it is unlikely that all these nations would default on their debts at once. On the other hand, a large portion of the money has been lent by relatively few banks to only a few major debtors. Default by Mexico and Brazil alone would wipe out 95 percent of the capital of the nine largest U.S. banks and 74 percent of the capital of the next 15 largest ones.

Such facts as these are enough to make sovereign risk credit a major item on the agenda of major international banks. Indeed in mid-1983 these banks were in the midst of a "second round" of financing talks with many of the debtors. Thus Nigeria reached a tentative agreement to convert $1.5 billion of arrears on letters of credit into a three-year loan. Peru was trying to stretch out more than $1.7 in foreign debts from one year to three years.

Brazil had been talking with the IMF about meeting the conditions required for domestic policy under an IMF loan agreed to in February 1983. At the same time it had been seeking more money from smaller European and American banks. Yugoslavia had been working with more than 500 banks on meeting its obligations. Chile had been trying to reschedule some $3.4 billion in loans from some 500 or 600 commercial banks, plus attempting to obtain some billions more in new money. Mexico proposed a plan to service some $1.5 billion of loans made by foreign banks to its private companies. Nicaragua wanted a deferment of $100 million due over 1983-84. The list goes on.

It is in Brazil, however, that the hastily stitched multibillion dollar financial bailouts for Latin American debtors are already unraveling. The Brazilian government announced in May 1983 that the IMF was withholding $411 million it was scheduled to pay Brazil on May 31, 1983 as the second installment on a $4.9 billion rescue loan granted in February 1983. The IMF was concerned about Brazil's failure to live up to its pledges to curb inflation, cut deficit spending, and carry out other belt-tightening measures.

Eventually, to avoid pushing Brazil into default, the IMF would probably have to part with the money anyway. But its reluctance signals the onset of a new and more dangerous stage in the third world debt crisis. The fund's delay would hold back Brazil's receipt of a $634 million installment on a $4.4 billion "jumbo" credit from commercial banks that was tied to the IMF loan. That would prevent

Brazil from meeting more than $700 million in payments to commercial banks and the Bank for International Settlements that would be falling due — added to $800 million in Brazilian debt payments that were already in arrears.

But, if the IMF disbursed the money to Brazil despite its failure to fulfill its promises, Mexico, Argentina, Peru, Chile, Yugoslavia, and other debtors in equally desperate straits would demand that the fund ease austerity measures imposed on them as a condition for getting similar bailouts.

The inability of Latin American debtors to meet their financial targets means they would need an additional infusion of $20 to $30 billion in 1983 and up to $30 billion in 1984 to keep them afloat, experts have predicted. Otherwise, they would almost certainly default.

The crisis left the biggest U.S. banks, which held $16.4 billion of Brazil's debt with little choice but to pump more money into Brazil. The United States, European, and Japanese commercial banks rolled over $4 billion of maturing Brazilian debt in February, 1983, besides lending $4.4 billion of new money.

But at the time of this writing (1983), regional American banks and European banks are refusing to renew interbank credits to Brazilian commercial banks. Interbank credits — very short-term loans from one bank to another — had already dropped to around $5.7 billion, which is $1.8 billion below the amount called for in the February, 1983 package, and the big U.S. money center banks will have to put up more funds to work further shrinkage. Since American banks have the largest exposure in Brazil many bankers feel that it is up to the larger American banks to buy out the smaller banks.

By May 1983 $600 million in interbank credits had been dropped by 40 to 50 U.S. regional banks, led by Dallas' Interfirst Corporation, the 14th-largest U.S. bank. European banks, mostly Swiss, French, and German, were putting pressure on the major U.S. banks by withholding more than $1 billion in interbank credits to Brazil.

There was, and continues to be, increasing disagreement among central banks about how the Brazilian crisis should be managed. The Bank of England — concerned about the $2 trillion Euromarket, based mostly in London — was backing U.S. efforts to keep Latin American debtors afloat. But Continental European central bankers were standing behind the technical arguments against including interbank credits in any rescheduling package and were instructing their major banks to hold out against pleas for help from the U.S. Treasury, the Federal Reserve Board, and the IMF.

Brazil's crisis is caused in part by unrealistic trade and financial projection used by banks, the IMF, and the Brazilian government as the basis for the initial hasty bail out. The rescue package was based on an estimated $6 billion Brazilian trade surplus in 1983 that was more likely to be around $4 billion.

As a result, Brazil would need an estimated $3 billion of new cash to get through 1983 and an additional $5 billion the next year. But there is growing talk in Brazil — most recently from several business associations — of calling a moratorium on debt payments rather than sinking deeper into debt. Whatever the outcome the main impact would be on the United States. The European central banks believe, in the end, that Brazil and other Latin American countries will become wards of the United States and if there is a default, they expect the Fed to step in and save the U.S. banks.

Is the international debt crisis a temporary cash crunch, which will fade with worldwide recovery, or is it an ever deepening hole out of which developing countries may never emerge?

According to a recent study by William Cline of the Institute for International Economics, the crisis is temporary — provided economic growth in industrialized countries averages at least 3 percent a year between 1984 and 1986.[1] Cline likens the difference to the insolvency-versus-liquidity debates that often surround corporate bankruptcy proceedings. If a firm's assets outweigh its liabilities but it is short of cash, then the firm is illiquid and usually manages to get additional loans, but if a firm's liabilities are greater than its assets, it is insolvent and will probably be unable to secure new loans.

According to Cline's study based on data from 19 countries which account for about two-thirds of the foreign debt of developing and Eastern European countries, the situation differs depending on assumptions used. Assuming 1.5 percent economic growth in 1983 and 3 percent a year from 1984 to 1986 in 24 nations that make up the OECD, Cline estimated that the current account deficit of the 19 debtor countries would drop to $48 billion in 1986 from $56 billion in 1982; that's $8 billion less that has to be externally financed. Cline figures the debtor countries will be able to raise the $48 billion.

Under the same assumption various measures of countries' creditworthiness such as debt payments as a percentage of export earnings, also improve.

Using his estimates Cline found wide variations among individual countries. A few examples: Between 1982 and 1986 Brazil's current account moves from a $14 billion deficit to $1.9 billion surplus; Korea's current account improves from a $2.2 billion deficit to a $10 billion surplus, and Chile's deficit widens from $2.5 to $4.7 billion. One of the biggest surprises is Venezuela's dismal showing; its current account deficit runs from $2.2 billion to $18.4 billion.

The study also looks at what might happen to the debt burden under various economic growth rates, interest rates, oil prices and dollar devaluations. For instance, if there is only 1 percent economic growth in 1983 followed by 1.5 percent annual growth from 1984 to 1986, the current account deficit of the 19 countries rises to a total of $102 billion in 1986 — an unmanageable figure. If interest rates average 13.5 percent instead of 8.75 percent, that boosts the current account deficit to $28 billion by 1986. And if the dollar stays strong, the overall credit worthiness of the debtor countries deteriorates because the dollar value of their exports decreases.

In all, according to Cline, a one percentage point change in the economic growth rates of the industrialized countries has four times the effect of a 10 percent change in the dollar, and five times the effect of a one percentage point change in interest rates.

Most surprising, according to Cline, is that falling oil prices worsen the debt crisis. This contradicts the view often expressed that sharply lower oil prices would tend to be good for developing countries and their debt problems because they are largely oil importers — but he adds that the major debtors as a group are oil exporters on balance.

The price of oil is certainly important to both the oil-producing and nonoil countries as well as to world banks. Amid the consensus of some oil experts that "OPEC has weathered the worst," other economists predict further price declines. They debate only how far oil prices might fall. Accordingly, commodity prices typically fall to the *cost of marginal production* which is the cost of adding new supplies. At this price producers no longer have an incentive to add new supplies and prices stabilize.

If we take this price as our guideline, oil prices could decline even more. The marginal cost of pumping oil from existing wells is 10 percent or less of the $29 that Saudi Arabia charges for a barrel of its Arabian light oil, the benchmark grade for OPEC. Once the wells are sunk and the fields are developed, operating costs are minimal. Indeed, oil can be taken out of the ground in the Mideast for as little as 50 cents per barrel. In Alaska it costs $2 to $5 per barrel.

The point is that supply is not likely to be responsive to price in the short-run so that prices can decline to their theoretical floor. This suggests that prices for oil can fall far before companies are inclined to cut production. Overcapacity in the oil industry makes such a development even more likely; OPEC can count only on its members' resolve to avoid. But there have been similar cartels in the past that have tried to control virtually every raw material. Most of them ultimately succumbed to price cutting.

Bankers are almost sure to lose as a result of a fall in the price of oil — at least in the short run. For although Brazil would easily repay its debts if oil prices fell and although some other countries and their balances of payments would join, Mexico and Venezuela in Latin America and Nigeria in Africa would not be able to stay the course. Indeed, these are the very countries which would precipitate a crash before the benefit of low oil prices was felt by the rest of the world.

Critics argue that Cline is too optimistic about the chances of 3 percent growth in future years, as well as the effects of such growth in developing countries' exports. Some economists and bankers also contend that Cline's assumptions guarantee his conclusions. They accuse him of ignoring political aspects of debt repayment. Even if current-account deficits are reduced, debtor countries may be unwilling to service debts for internal political reasons.

Others think the insolvency-liquidity approach is too simplistic. Whether you get an insolvency or liquidity conclusion, you are still going to need tremendous amounts of money for these countries for the next several years.

This is also suggested by other studies. For instance, preliminary results reported in studies made by the staff of the Federal Reserve board of governors that the debt burden, as uncovered by ratio of real interest payments to exports, rose significantly in 1982 for eight developing-debtor countries studied, though it is expected to decline through 1990.[2] The countries studied are Mexico, Brazil, Venezuela, Korea, Chile, Philippines, and Peru. According to these studies the debt burden would be reduced rapidly by reductions of real interest rates or equivalent changes in the present value of outstanding debts. More rapid economic growth in the industrial countries, and thus an increase in export earnings of developing-debtor countries, provide a powerful effect by 1990 but not over the shorter term. A similar effect holds for policies adopted by developing-debtor countries that result in larger trade surpluses.

PROPOSED SOLUTIONS

The strategy of Tit for Tat calls for continued cooperation on the parts of banks and others. Its guidelines are: Don't be envious, don't be first to defect, reciprocate both defection and cooperation, and don't be too clever. Consider now proposed solutions to the debt issue against the background of our theory of cooperation and its guidelines. Suppose, in fact, the worst case scenario is realized and debtor countries can neither service nor pay their debt obligations. This indeed came uncomfortably close to realization in the autumn of 1982. It was only prevented from happening by emergency aid from the Bank for International Settlements and the U.S. Treasury, quickly followed by the IMF which required policy changes from Mexico and other debtors in return for cash. The IMF then prevailed upon banks to reschedule their loans and provide new ones. It is doubtful that such an operation can be repeated and carried out successfully.

This has prompted discussion of several proposals for handling poor countries' debts. One such proposal is a secondary market in converted bank loans. Another is to allow the IMF to create a so-called compensatory financing facility (CFF). A third is to increase the IMF quotas. Central banks could, for instance, promote a secondary market in converted bank loans. Any bank that wanted to move assets off its books could then agree to new terms with the borrower and put the package up for sale. Everything has a price. Some debt collectors specialize in buying out bad debts. Given time, an international market would develop.

The IMF has long had a compensatory financing facility (CFF) that makes loans to commodity exporters if their foreign-exchange earnings fall because of factors beyond their control. It is argued that a similar arrangement can be made for an interest rate CFF on the logic that high American interest rates have taken much more out of the export earnings of some big borrowers than commodity disasters. If they were compensated for higher interest charges, they could be required to pass the extra money through to their bankers. An interest rate CFF could replace some of the IMF's standard lending, while retaining its conditionality. If more money is needed, the IMF can then go to the markets.

The third measure advanced is for the governments of the major industrial countries to become more actively engaged in resolving the debt crisis. This includes increasing the IMF quota. The increased U.S. contribution, for instance, would amount to $8.4 billion which includes $5.8 billion for the IMF's regular lending resources and $2.6 billion for an emergency fund to serve as a backstop for cash-squeezed countries whose possible default could threaten the world financial system.

The American share was part of an international plan to increase the 146 country organization's lending resources 47.7 percent by the end of 1983 to $98.5 billion from the then current $66.8 billion. The IMF planned to enlarge a separate $7.1 billion fund to $19 billion to serve as the emergency fund.

Another proposal discussed in *The Economist* (April 30, 1983) and put forward by an international banker, M. Zombanakis, suggests that countries rescheduling their debts should make 13 year agreements with the IMF. Normal commercial bank lending to these countries could then resume, for projects that accorded with their new IMF guarantee. This guarantee provides that if a borrower had fulfilled all IMF conditions for 10 years and still failed to be able to repay its debts, then the IMF itself would guarantee the repayments of the debts in years 11 to 13. Meeting IMF conditions which require a shift of resources to export-oriented industries and a minimum of populist politics and programs would presumably provide adequate insurance that few countries would fail to meet their obligations.

The Economist in discussing the above proposal prefers a system with graduated deterrents including a secondary market in international bad debts. The idea is that commercial banks would put a defaulting country X promises to repay up for sale, and these promises would rise in market price as and if country X came near to restoring its creditworthiness by qualifying for IMF guarantee.

There are several problems with the Zombanakis rescheduling proposal. In the first place, there is no guarantee that some of these countries, if allowed to borrow for projects approved by the new IMF arrangements, would indeed spend all the money on the designated projects. It is likely that there would be a diversion of funds to other less meritorious projects as has happened in the past in many developing countries. In the second place, the IMF is not equipped to deal with the internal debt situations created by companies both private and public who have succeeded in borrowing well in excess of the amounts needed for normal fixed and working capital financing to finance operating losses and financial charges. Domestic and International banks have sustained these excesses in borrowing. Finally, the proposal fails to deal with the situation if debtor countries simply refuse to play by the rules of the game. If they refuse, the question will not be international liquidity to less-developed countries but the solvency of international lending. This calls eventually for the creation of an international lender of last resort and large-scale international monetary reform.

An IMF-based approach may be the correct way to resolve the macroeconomic maladjustments. But the IMF approach is less well equipped to resolve the internal debt problem since this involves forcing a painful micro-level adjustment on those corporations which have so far preferred debt accumulation to genuine adjustment (realistic public enterprise pricing is by no means the only example). The standard IMF approach is unlikely to affect this adjustment although it may certainly change the nature of the internal debt problem.

First, by realistic exchange-rate and interest-rate policies it may discourage the flight of capital and so raise the deposit base of the domestic banks to sustain higher levels of domestic spending. Second, by calming the foreign banks it may encourage the supply of future external bank finance to the corporations and so help to support excessive debt in certain corporations for a bit longer.

Third, it will further raise the nominal and possible real interest rates to indebted companies and raise their demands on the credit system yet higher. Finally, though the deflation will accompany macro-adjustment, it will exacerbate the operating positions of already distressed companies and so add to their credit demands.

However well designed a macroeconomic stabilization package may be, it is difficult to see how the associated credit instrument can be designed to have most impact on the least efficient companies (the incentive to borrow, especially at high real interest rates, will be greatest in those companies whose equity is already virtually wiped out). It is also difficult to see how to avoid high real interest rates which can damage efficient companies.

The evidence suggests that a macro-adjustment has to be combined with operations to reconstruct the capital base parts of the corporate sector as well as significant reform of banking and financial institutions in the borrowing countries. Without it we may merely be papering cracks. These issues will be discussed in the following chapters.

The Economist (May 21, 1983, p. 14) suggests that

> . . . Any debtor asking to reschedule should be judged by three tests. Has it changed its ways? Is the change showing results? Are those results producing bankable cash? Lags are unavoidable: policy changes will not bring instant rewards, much though nervous money men push for such reassurance. Nor can changes be spun out over several years, as unhappy debtors would like. Somewhere in between lies the ground for compromise. Rescheduling touched that ground last autumn [1982] but now looks like leaving it.
>
> . . . Hence the ever greater importance of making sure that domestic policies are being changed to promote exports and domestic savings. This remains the IMF's job and one where it should not be too lenient. . . . The IMF's emphasis on changing the policies of its borrowers will be compromised if it is expected to be permissive and stern at the same time. Having rightly persuaded the banks to lend more to the Brazils and the Mexicos on the promise of policy change, the IMF will lose credibility if it does not enforce its side of the bargain. And a creditable IMF is about all that stands between here and the abyss.

Another proposal is provided by Lord Lever, an advisor to the British Labor party government of 1974-79.[3] Accordingly, governments must act collectively to support the over-borrowed developing countries and the over-strained banking system. The Lever plan proposes to extend the role of export agencies to include sovereign loan guarantees. Through the extended role of existing agencies there would be a sort of worldwide agency acting upon IMF advice which would advise the export agencies on country risk matters relating to balance of payments loans.

Banks would be advised against making "unproductive" loans. The assumption is, evidently, that there are many "productive" investments in many developing countries which are waiting to be made, if only banks were given the proper advice. To judge from the scattered evidence presented by various aid and credit agencies this may not be correct. They find that there are very few projects that would not take a much longer time to recover their costs than banks or credit agencies would accommodate. Most of the exceptions, in fact, are to be found in such "colonial" investments as natural resource development.

Export credit agencies of individual countries, moreover, are notoriously parochial in support of national industries. They may well push so-called marginal projects in developing countries simply on behalf of their home constituents. An insured credit to cover "reasonable" current-account deficit would be available to each central bank in debtor countries and thus be likely to provide the incentive.

Still another proposal made by some private investment bankers (for example, B. Mohr of New York, *The Economist* July 30, 1983, p. 1) would transfer all existing sovereign loans to the IMF after a phased-in write-off of truly unrecoverable loans over a period of time. Sovereign lending then would become the sole responsibility of the IMF which would gain access to the international money markets. Its quotas would have to be increased substantially and more than presently envisioned. There would also be a transfer of technical staff from major American and foreign banks to the IMF. No longer would ministers of finance face hundreds of bankers; instead they would deal only with representatives from IMF.

This transfer is not viewed as a bail-out of banks. It is, according to its sponsors, a restoration of world order. With the disappearance of the balance-of-payments loans from the banks' balance sheets, real interest rates will fall; borrowing nations will tie their external debt to export revenues in a more disciplined fashion; and finally, the risk to which the individual taxpayer is exposed is reduced, the sovereign risk no longer having the threat of massive write off.

Other proposals are also available. Many share the view that, if governments are asked to make more credits available to the debtor countries either directly or through various international agencies, banks must limit their interest and fees from these loans and deposit the income in loan-loss reserves rather than pay it out as dividends. Nor should the banks receive interest or principal payments before any agency financed by the taxpayers.

The banks and their shareholders must accept real risk as the counterpart to their profits from foreign lending. Otherwise even the specter of an international financial crisis will not persuade the taxpayers of many countries to keep either foreign debtors or their bank creditors afloat.

Numerous other proposals for longer-term solutions abound. Most of these proposals concern the recycling of international banks' troubled assets, either through one of the established international agencies (such as the I.M.F. or World Bank) or a newly created international financial intermediary. The main idea is to relieve banks of their high risk loans in order to minimize their losses, to limit financial uncertainties, and to free bank funds for lubricating the wheels of a worldwide recovery.

It is, moreover, regretable that in the discussion about rescuing the debtor countries there is not more talk about equity investment, free markets, enterprise, economic discipline, and political responsibility. Several of these countries' leaders impose their versions of authoritarianism or socialism or indeed democracy on their societies, encouraging the creation of inefficient bureaucracies, inefficient over-controlled systems, and more distortions of internal markets. Added to this, in some countries bribery and corruption are important negative factors. None of these elements can be set right by providing such countries with additional loans. Any country, of course, is free to indulge in its fantasies and utopias. There is no reason for world banks, however, to provide the finance.

There is considerable disagreement over a number of these proposed measures to ease the debt issue. In particular, suggestions to expand IMF's role and/or quotas are not received by everyone as constructive. Indeed, there is disagreement if in fact there is an international "debt crisis." These critics charge that as conventionally defined, the international debt crisis is for all practical purposes over with the end of the severe recession in 1983.

Accordingly, it is the "unexpectedly" severe recession that is the chief element in the debt crisis.[4] And some bankers agree. To be sure the less developed countries were finding it more difficult to export their goods to industrialized countries and thereby generate enough revenue to meet their debt service. The length and severity of the recession supposedly made it necessary to arrange an emergency fund to stave off an old-fashioned banking panic. This was done in 1982.

Moreover, if a crisis really does exist, so the argument goes, the IMF already has $45 billion of gold that could be pledged to raise more than enough hard currency to deal with it. Furthermore, the proposed quota increase would not take place until late in 1983. This is hardly the emergency cited by proponents of a need to increase IMF quotas. The "debt crisis" is apparently being used as a means for permanently augmenting the power of the IMF bureaucracy. This is what we should expect according to our theory of bureaucracy.

There is, in addition, a confidential Federal Reserve/Treasury Staff study made in the summer of 1982 which concluded, according to the *Wall Street Journal*, that "a collapse of the system is highly unlikely (although) there is always the danger that an individual borrower, or borrowing country, will run into difficulties." Only in the cases of Mexico and Brazil, the study said, "is the magnitude of U.S. banks' exposure sufficient to pose a potential threat to confidence in the event of total loss." But the study quickly added, reports the *Wall Street Journal*, "total loss . . . is highly unlikely."[5]

It is thus incumbent on those arguing in favor of a quota increase for the IMF to show why in fact large sums should be taken out of the capital markets of the United States and other primarily industrial countries, guaranteed by taxpayers, and passed on to countries with demonstrated records of poor economic policies. Neither is it clear, argue the skeptics, why adding more debt to the backs of poor debtor countries will help rather than hurt them. Or how it will help the soundness of the banking system to be "bailed in" for billions more in shaky loans to whomever the IMF's bureaucrats deem worthy. The IMF, to be sure, has had some success in recent years. Many of its customers, unfortunately, have become regulars coming back again and again for more money.

Furthermore, some debtor nations, bankers and IMF officials, and others have a vested interest in "bailouts". It should be no surprise that such specters as a $600 billion-plus debt owed to industrialized countries by the non-OPEC developing countries is used by these vested interests to scare the public. Only a fraction of that total, however, is in doubt and that amount will be reduced by the economic recovery which began in 1983. Indeed, banks themselves, argue the skeptics, seem in no hurry to raise their reserves substantially against the calamity supposedly stalking them.

As a matter of fact, however, most European international banks have been increasing reserves to cover any losses should any of their loans to Eastern Europe and developing countries go sour. It is thus difficult to estimate just how well covered European banks actually are, because they are free to put away hidden reserves as well as those made in the public books. But it is believed they may well have piled up more reserves than American banks. For instance, the German Commerzbank paid no dividend in 1982 despite sharply higher earnings so as to build up reserves for this purpose. It was expected to do the same in 1983.

Some banks are, in fact, accommodating to the debt circumstances of their host countries by investing their local currency loan profits in favored sectors of the economy.[6] In the process these banks are making very respectable rates of profit indeed. For instance, Citibank earned $153 million, or 20 percent of its worldwide income in Brazil and Chase Manhattan Bank — through its 98 percent-owned subsidiary Banco Lar — made $25 million from local cruzeiro business. Along with the First National Bank of Boston they are the only foreigners owning local banks. They are permitted to lend cruzeiros at annual rates as high as 205 percent. The cruzeiro business not only yields significant profits but also protects them from the hard currency liquidity crisis common to Latin America.

Whatever their individual merits and limitations the proposed solutions thus far discussed do provide ideas and elements that can be drawn upon and incorporated into a more general approach to the relations between debtor and creditor nations which is at the same time consistent with the guidelines of our theory of cooperation with reciprocity and a Tit for Tat strategy. These elements include banks, rescheduling of debt, central banks, monetary authorities, private individuals, and the IMF. The ideas include the steps for qualifying a debtor country for rescheduling loans and in some instances "writing down" loans and creating secondary markets for such loans as outlined by *The Economist* and discussed in this chapter.

Accordingly, banks would continue their primary role in the debtor-creditor relationship. We have discussed their "cluster" role in our theory of cooperation. In order to strengthen their ability to do so bank authorities must improve the regulatory atmosphere in which banks operate. This is also correct for debtor-developing countries as well. These issues are discussed in our next chapters.

Rescheduling of loans is the market's way of dealing with a debt crisis. It produces benefits for both banks and debtors. There is no need for banks to write off problem loans. Debtor nations avoid the unpopular consequences of default. There is no need for "bail-outs" or "write-offs" of debtor nation loans. Rescheduling of loans is within the guidelines of our theory. It is a mechanism for assuring an iterative game. The players are forced to meet regularly.

Currently a debtor nation calls upon the IMF when it discovers a foreign exchange shortage. The IMF then sends a *mission* to determine what steps the nation should take to regain economic well-being, and those steps are defined in a *conditionality* agreement. If the debtor nation accepts these conditions it gets a direct IMF loan. Far more important, however, it also gets access to the world's private credit markets. The IMF then monitors the debtor country's adherence to these agreements. In the event problems develop, the IMF responds with a threat to suspend loan payments, the private sector very quickly follows, and negotiations begin again.

The steps for rescheduling suggested by *The Economist* incorporates, basically, our cooperative strategy with reciprocity of Tit for Tat. Three tests would be applied to the debtor country asking for rescheduling. First, has the debtor country actually changed its ways? Second, are changes showing results? Third, are those results in fact bringing in "bankable cash"? Since policy changes do not bring immediate results, allowances must be made for lags. On the other hand, policy changes which unnecessarily stretch out efforts over many years can not be accepted within the strategy of Tit for Tat. There is, however, room for a compromise between these extremes.

In addition to making sure that domestic policies are being changed to promote exports and domestic savings, the IMF plays another constructive role in the rescheduling process. It provides the processor or arena in which players meet and the tournament is played. Under the proposed arrangement the IMF mediates differences between debtor and creditor nations within a Tit for Tat strategy. There is no need for it to give money to debtors to do this. In fact, giving money is likely to prevent some necessary rescheduling adjustments as both debtors and creditors would be less likely to compromise. In effect, giving money is simply increasing the incentive to defect from the game. There is thus no need to expand the financial capacity of the fund for this purpose. There is also no need to expand central control of the international monetary and financial system. The strategy of Tit for Tat will work in promoting and establishing a cooperative environment.

Under this scheme, the IMF can be viewed as an important credit-rating agency, a political Standard & Poor's. It provides credit assessment necessary if banks and private organizations are to continue foreign lending.

One can also argue that incorporation of the Standard & Poor's model to foreign lending makes the IMF redundant. Like any private concern Standard & Poor's sells its product in our example credit assessments in an open market. Since private, Standard & Poor's only rates securities but does not lend as does the IMF. Accordingly, it does not have a conflict problem of simultaneously rating a country's securities and holding them. It does not have an incentive to avoid any downgrading that would reduce the value of its own holdings. In effect, the private sector Standard & Poor's leaves the business of lending to others, which leaves it free to give forthright evaluations. It is, moreover, self financed. That is, the costs of rating and monitoring various debt issues are paid by the concerns or governments issuing the debt.

Another private market financial evaluation instrument used extensively during the internal struggle for monetary supremacy in the United States during the turbulent 1830s and 1840s is the *banknote detector*. The vari-valued (in specie) notes of early commercial banks in the United States provoked the logical and useful business of bank note detection. A commercial publication developed and used by the prudent in the pre-National Bank Act era was the banknote detector, a form of trade journal published weekly by specialists on the subject and used by every businessman and banker whose receipts were in bank notes. The notes of hundreds of banks circulated in any community. Each of them had some monetary prestige. Some were as good as specie; some were worth one-half the face value; and some were counterfeit. In fact, the difference between a "legitimate" paper issue and a counterfeit issue was one of degree and not of kind. The discount on a particular issue in part expressed the degree of difference. Matters were further complicated by the fact that the more dubious an issue of bank notes the more likely the notes would not be loaned out in the vicinity of the issuing bank, but used to purchase merchandise far from home for resale at a profit. The merchant to whom one of these notes was offered, if unskilled in exchange, had little choice but to take it upon some terms. In order to determine the bank notes that were valid, and if valid, the approximate worth in gold and silver, the merchant turned to his *detector*. In December 1842, for example, Bicknell's Counterfeit Bank Note Detector, in addition to providing current economic intelligence, reported that notes of some banks in the several states were worth 50 cents per dollar of specie.[7]

As in the Standard and Poor's method the detector can be adopted on a worldwide scale to provide necessary information for evaluating individual projects and security issues of active and failed organizations. Instead of checking the specie validity of bank notes the instrument now could be used to check the ongoing economic and market validity of various debt-financed investment projects in developing-debtor nations.

World banks and/or other private organizations with established country relations already collect much of the necessary information for the detector as a part of their on-going activities. The information could be made available as a commercial publication and sold to interested individuals and organizations. Such information would be very useful to banks and others particularly in cases where banks have difficulty in saying no to additional loans to customers whose record of performance on existing loans is judged less than satisfactory.

The *project and security detector* could serve a secondary market in developing-debtor country debt instruments along the lines suggested in our earlier discussion. For instance, an international market for bad debts can develop given time. One can envision specialists in such markets providing the necessary debt-collecting services for a price in much the same fashion as earlier American bank note brokers.

A secondary market in the debt of developing-debtor countries can be secured by the IMF, World Bank, or a new entity providing a conduit role by buying the bank loans made to various developing-debtor countries, pooling them, and selling participation interests in the pools. A model for such an arrangement is provided by the American Federal Home Loan Mortgage Corporation, a quasi-government agency which developed an efficient secondary market in conventional home mortgages.[8]

Such an arrangement provides a mechanism by which investors other than banks actively engaged in international banking can buy, and sell foreign loans. This would be facilitated by the debt instruments traded which would consist of a limited number of homogeneous categories employing standardized documents. At the same time, the arrangement leaves intact the strategic advantage banks possess in originating foreign loans by virtue of their investment in information and the capacity to generate information sources. In addition, it also leaves intact the incentive for banks to monitor and control loan risk. In effect, the "cluster" role for banks is preserved as earlier.

Another proposal for a secondary market provides for marketable consol certificates with prior claim. It is aimed at countries undergoing debt-servicing problems. Essentially, the new money would be raised in the market by issuing floating rate consol certificates with prior claim over all old debt. The IMF and World Bank would approve the issue of such consols and an amount would be held by either the IMF or World Bank. It would be the Fund's responsibility to monitor and control the consols until they are retired.

The arrangement would assure a continued but monitored flow of credit to the developing-debtor countries in difficulty. It thus reinforces the incentive not to adopt a non-nice strategy and defect from our tournament. Given their high quality, volume, and homogeneity the new consol would also attract additional lenders and thus increase the number of participants in the tournament favorably disposed to cooperation with a Tit for Tat strategy.

The old and existing debt can be handled in a similar manner by having the portion owed or guaranteed by the government of the developing-debtor country acquire it by the issuance of free-floating consols, one for each of the currencies in which its old debt is denominated. The consols would be guaranteed by the country's central bank or similar organization. For each of the currency-denominated consols the spread would be a penalty rate set as a minimum at the highest level of any of the old spreads.[9] Private debt would be left to arrangements between borrower and lender.

The arrangement is consistent with the guidelines of our theory of cooperation. It decreases the liquidity burden and thus the incentive to defect on the part of the developing-debtor country by eliminating the need to repay principal. However, it increases the real debt burden because of the increased penalty interest rate. In effect, the continuity of the game is assured in that long run solvency of the developing-debtor country is assured while at the same time providing an incentive for the country to repay as quickly as possible.

In our game it is essential that domestic monetary authorities and central banks maintain monetary stability and furnish an elastic currency. They must keep the money supply from contracting in the event of a run on their banks. They must assure that the monetary system itself is not a source of instability. By doing both they assure that an evolving environment of cooperation with reciprocity will not be aborted. Our historical episodes provide ample evidence on the consequences of policy failures in these areas. We shall have more to say on monetary stability elsewhere in this study.

NOTES

1. Reported in *Wall Street Journal* May 26, 1983, p. 34.
2. See, for instance, M. Dooley, W. Helkie, R. Tryon and J. Underwood, "An Analysis of External Debt Positions of Eight Developing Countries Through 1990", *International Finance Discussion Papers* No. 227, August, 1983.
3. "The Lever Plan", *The Economist* July 9, 1983, pp. 15-16. See also the study by Robert E. Weintraub, *The International Debt; Crisis and Challenge* (Fairfax: George Mason University, 1983); G. G. Johnson with Richard K. Agrams *Aspects of the International Banking Safety Net* (Washington: International Monetary Fund, 1983, Occasional paper 17). Jack Guttentag and Richard Herring, "Overexposure of International Banks to Country Risk: Diagnosis and Remedies," Paper prepared for the Committee on Banking, Finance and Urban Affairs of the House of Representatives and presented at hearings on April 20, 1983, and at International Finance Division Federal Reserve Board Seminar, July 13, 1983, Washington, D.C.
4. See for example, "What Debt Crisis?" *Wall Street Journal*, April 20, 1983, p. 30. See also Robert E. Weintraub, *The International Debt: Crisis and Challenge* (Fairfax: George Mason University, 1983); *Key Issues in International Banking*, Federal Reserve Bank of Boston, Conference Series No. 18 (1978).
5. Op. cit. (note 4).
6. "How Foreign Banks Still Get Rich in Brazil," *Business Week*, August 22, 1983, p. 102.
7. Advertisements for the notes of broken banks appeared regularly in the financial sections because these notes could be used as claims against the existing capital of the broken banks. Thus Bicknell continually issued the following form. In 1835 he advertised:

"Broken Bank Notes Wanted"
The subscriber having received on order for the following sum in notes of Broken Banks, will purchase same, in lots, at the following prices:

$5,000 Bank of Maryland	at $.20 on the dollar
4,000 Susquehanna Bridge payable at Md. Savings Inst.	at .40 on the dollar
1,000 Bank of Alexandria	at .80 on the dollar
500 Bank of New Brunswick	at .20 on the dollar
500 Farmer's Bank	at .30 on the dollar
500 Salisbury Bank	at .50 on the dollar
250 Comm. Bank Milling	at .90 on the dollar
250 Westmoreland Bank	at .75 on the dollar

Robert T. Bicknell
No. 2 Philadelphia Exchange

Bicknell's *Counterfeit Detector*, Vol. III, No. 1, April 1835.

Indeed, there is currently developing a new market in exchanging high risk debt similar to the early American bank note brokers. To be sure swapping does little if anything to solve the overall debt problem, which is to keep interest and debt payments flowing from nearly bankrupt countries. But debt swaps, in which U.S. and foreign banks exchange country credits, are growing. Regulators and bankers estimate that about $1 billion has changed hands already, and an active market is expanding.

The incentive for such swaps is that they allow banks to reduce concentration of risk to one country and fix up their balance sheets without taking write-downs that Congress and some regulators are demanding. Moreover, loans that are swapped have to be priced at market value. Swaps are creating the first priced-based comparison of the creditworthiness of high risk-country debtors.

According to *Business Week*, December 5, 1983 (p. 144), in recent trades, for instance, Brazilian debt sold for 72 cents to 75 cents on the dollar, Mexican for 85 cents, Venezuelan 80 cents to 85 cents, and Argentine for 77 cents to 80 cents. As in the early American state bank note detector era, the merging market is setting actual values on what sovereign-risk debt is worth, based on cash transactions.

8. See J. Guttentag and R. Herring, op. cit., pp. 17-20.

9. Guttentag and Herring (Ibid., p. 23) go farther and suggest that the value of these consols would be adjusted on the books of bankholders by writing them down 1 percent every month that the country's interest payment is delinquent. In effect, in 100 months the consols would be freely written off the holder's books if the country pays no interest.

5.

CHANGING ANATOMY OF BANKING

INTRODUCTION

This study underscores the need to strengthen banks. One means for doing so is to admit more competition into the banking industry. There is now reason to believe that the regulatory atmosphere in the United States and elsewhere is changing to admit the competitive and transnational character of banking.[1] The umbrella of protection is being removed from banking. It is expected that the discipline of the market will lead to a stronger, safer and more stable banking system. The banking industry has been viewed as "special" for too long. More market orientation will lead to a banking industry capable of servicing a more interdependent world as we move into the twenty-first century. The anatomy of banking is changing. How it is changing and some of the underlying factors promoting change are discussed in this chapter.

CHANGING REGULATORY ENVIRONMENT

What is a bank? This is a question that is repeatedly being asked by regulators and legislative bodies as distinctions between financial institutions blur. Congress has discussed the question many times in the past with little definitive resolution. The Glass-Steagall Act passed in the 1930s attempted to keep such financial institutions as banks and brokers apart. And in the 1830s Congress and the administration attempted to keep separate "money" from bank notes and deposits. Neither effort can be called an unqualified success.

Two proposals are before Congress at this writing: the financial institutions holding company deregulations bill would allow all depository institutions — commercial banks, savings and loan associations, and savings banks — to expand through holding companies so that they can compete fully with financial service groups. This would include areas from which they are now barred, such as insurance, property development, and brokerage and investment banking. Banks would have to conduct such business through their parent company so that depositors could be protected and so that banks could not use their access to cheaper money to gain an edge on financial service companies.

The U.S. Treasury sees it as an unstoppable but welcome deregulation wave which is sweeping through the American banking industry.

The American Federal Reserve Board on the other hand, is not as enthusiastic about this free market trend. The Board believes that banks are special and so need special regulation. There have to be restrictions on diversification in order to protect depositors. Although it accepts that it cannot now do much about banks buying into discount brokerage firms, the Federal Reserve is attempting to block creation of so-called nonbank banks (limited purpose banks). These are institutions that have taken advantage of loopholes in the law. By giving up their right to make commercial loans — one of the legal characteristics of a bank — they can become both a bank, thereby qualifying them for Federal Deposit Insurance and a nonbank thereby allowing them the freedom to offer unregulated services.

Indeed following the "Dreyfus Affair" in the New York money market, the Federal Reserve has broadened its definition of a "deposit," which is another legal characteristic of a bank, to draw such institutions within its regulatory jurisdiction. It has also called for a moratorium on any further "financial innovation" until Congress has worked out where it wants to go.

Agreeing with the Treasury view that the government neither can, nor should, halt the pace at which the financial marketplace is changing are the Federal Deposit Insurance Corporation and the big banks and other financial groups in the marketplace, the FDIC because institutional deregulation would give it a larger role. For their part the smaller banks and financial institutions do not view freer competition as necessarily to their advantage. For the purposes at hand, competition will strengthen the ability of banks to play their important role in both domestic and international finance. The system is not working to achieve desired ends under the present regulatory regime. Old regulations are patched up and new ones are added, with the effect of inducing new means of avoidance. The means of avoidance for instance involve the creation of uninsured liabilities that are used as money. This in turn adds to the problems of the monetary authorities and central banks in preserving monetary stability so important to the issues of banks and debt under discussion in this book.

BUSINESS OF BANKING

Contemporary commercial banks may be described as financial department stores.[2] Although banks provide many services to the community, their principal business is the lending and investing of money and handling deposits. This is their stock in trade. In peddling their wares commercial banks attempt to maximize their returns in a manner similar to all other profit-making concerns in the private sector of the economy.

There are two types of returns that a businessman will consider in running his or another's business concern and indeed that an individual will take into account in choosing an occupation. They are pecuniary returns and nonpecuniary returns.

Pecuniary returns are the most easily understood in that they are quantifiable. The information is provided by wage rates, incomes, or from the financial statements of business concerns. The latter for the most part indicate clearly the size of the monetary return that the business organization has managed to obtain from the sale of its products. Nonpecuniary returns, however, are more elusive because they are not readily quantifiable.

In the case of an individual confronted with an occupational choice, for example, nonpecuniary returns depend on his tastes and preferences in evaluating the nonmonetary advantages or disadvantages of an occupation. A steady but modest monetary income with congenial coworkers is preferred by some people to the preferences of others for large pecuniary incomes obtainable in more disagreeable surroundings. Similarly, a businessman may prefer a take-things-easy attitude and so a modest monetary return for his organization to the greater exertion that a larger pecuniary return would require. A banker may prefer the easy life that safety of greater liquidity offers to the pecuniary income that he will lose through this attitude. And, in fact, moderate but consistent monetary returns are a characteristic of the banking business.

In their attempts to allocate available bank funds to maximize monetary and nonmonetary returns, bankers as businessmen must solve the double problems of liquidity and solvency. At the same time, these problems must be solved within limitations imposed by legal considerations. The amount of liquidity actually needed by an individual bank is of fundamental importance. Too much liquidity means that the bank is foregoing pecuniary returns and thus may not earn what is considered a normal return, so that stockholders will permanently withdraw their funds from the bank and employ them elsewhere where such a return, or a better one, is obtainable. Too little liquidity, on the other hand, may be fatal to the life of a bank and perhaps disturbing to the banker's peace of mind.

Important as liquidity is to a bank as a going concern it alone cannot guarantee solvency. In this matter banks are not different from other businesses. Thus a business may be liquid enough to meet all its liabilities currently due and for which payment is demanded, and still be insolvent. To be solvent a business concern must, at a minimum, possess assets whose total value is as great as the sum of its liabilities to outsiders. And finally, legal considerations in the past imposed restrictions on the monetary returns that a bank may earn by limiting its holdings of certain categories of earning assets and excluding others.

INPUT "MIX"[3]

As distinct from other businesses, commercial banks take pride in their debt obligations to the public. It is simply a fact that if bankers had to depend upon their own capital there would indeed be very few banks on the contemporary scene. Deposits (demand and time) are the chief ingredients in the input "mix" of banks. They are used to manufacture the industry's principal product, which is bank credit.

One source of these deposits is the public's surrender of cash to the bank. The second source is the granting of loans and making investments. The first are known as primary deposits and the second as derived deposits. Individual bankers view derived deposits as tending to reduce their cash reserves and so they encourage an increase in primary deposits as a means of enabling them to increase their loan-created (or investment-created) derived deposits. Thus, they attempt to increase confidence in their institution by advertising their debt obligations to present depositors, thereby hoping to encourage others to make deposits with them.

The type and nature of the deposit liabilities to the public are important determinants of a bank's input mix. Commercial bank deposits in the United States may be classified broadly into demand, time, and savings deposits and subclassified according to the nature of the depositor: (1) private individuals, partnerships, and corporations; (2) states and political subdivisions; (3) United States government; and (4) foreign.

It is generally agreed that classification of deposits according to the functions that they perform does not yield clear lines of demarcation. Demand deposits are typically held for purposes of making payments. Time and savings deposits are an investment outlet for individual savers. There is, however, considerable interchange in the uses to which the various types of accounts are put thereby blurring the lines drawn between their functions. In addition, banks in practice seldom exercise their right to require advance notice of withdrawals from time and savings deposits by their customers.

As in many other industries, commercial banking is not assured of a steady source of supply for its principal inputs. Private individuals who own and use demand deposits for personal convenience are the most numerous class of demand depositors. A banker can depend on regular withdrawals by this class of depositor. This source of supply, normally, will not cause a banker much concern. Far more important to banks in terms of dollar volume are the deposits of business. Since many businesses have special seasonal and cyclical characteristics, a banker must anticipate and prepare for these deposit withdrawals by adjusting his investment portfolios so as to provide the required amount of liquidity. This may reduce the output of his principal product, namely, loans.

Local, state, and national government deposits are another source of particular concern to bankers because receipts and expenditures by various levels of government are not synchronized. For instance, at certain times of the year when taxes are collected, deposits in public accounts increase substantially and decline in other times when expenditures are heavy. Since coincidence between the deposits of taxpayers and recipients of government checks cannot be counted upon by an individual bank, bankers attempt to offset the public accounts they hold by a high degree of liquidity in their assets and so reduce loan output.

The behavior of foreign deposits is perhaps the least predictable. Their behavior is influenced by a wide range of foreign and domestic factors. Bankers are not readily disposed to use these funds in other than highly liquid activities. Most of these accounts are carried by commercial banks in New York and other money centers.

Other major sources of bank funds, and so ingredients in a bank's input mix, are its own capital, including surplus, individual profits and reserves for losses, and funds borrowed from other banks and the Federal Reserve System.

OUTPUT "MIX"

Loans

Although investments and loans are both important "products" of commercial banks, loans are their primary form of output. A banker with a decided preference for pecuniary returns, will, ceteris paribus, also prefer this type of output because of its higher pecuniary return. Loan output "mix" consists of short-term commercial loans, term loans, real estate loans, consumer loans, and security loans.

Business firms are the major customers for short-run commercial loans. Demand for this type of loan is very sensitive to economic fluctuations rising during the upswing of economic activity when business is prosperous, and declining in the down-swing. Coupled with its cyclical sensitivity is its seasonal variation. There is a tendency for business to increase its bank borrowing to finance the processing of the year's crop and to prepare for holiday shopping. There is also a tendency for business borrowing from banks to be directly related to inventory fluctuations. Inventory buildup or depletion will tend to be reflected in business borrowing.

Term loans are usually sought by businesses that are too small to use capital markets, or by larger firms that prefer to seek term credit from banks rather than to sell their securities. And, indeed, some loans that are classified as short term because they are renewed periodically, are in fact used by borrowers to finance permanent working-capital requirements so that they are in effect term loans.

Real estate loans in the form of farm and nonfarm mortgages tend to be the province of small banks. Such loans are a minor output of large commercial banks. Demand for this type of loan appears to be independent of moderate movements in general economic activity. Residential construction tends to depend mainly upon family formation, population growth, and population shifts. Commercial construction on the other hand is more closely related to movements in general economic activity. Farm mortgages tend to be closely associated with the purchase of land, which is influenced by the movement of agricultural prices.

Consumer loans are another important element in the output mix of commercial banks. Moreover, banks meet consumer demands for loans also in an indirect manner. They finance consumers indirectly through loans to dealers in durable goods, sales finance companies, as well as other lending agencies. These loans tend to conform closely to movements in general economic activity. In addition, they appear to be affected by the willingness of consumers to increase their debt, which in turn appears to be influenced by evaluation of their past and future incomes.

Security loans are another element in a bank's loan output mix. These loans fall into broad categories: (1) "Street loans," for example, brokers and dealers in securities; (2) loans made to others for the purpose of carrying securities. This type of lending constitutes an important element in the output mix of banks located in the country's principal financial centers. For most other banks in the country, however, this type of loan is a minor element in their loan output. Demand for security loans is affected primarily by changes in stock prices, current margin requirements in stocks and general new security offerings, prevailing rates on security loans, and on speculative activity in the securities markets.

Investment Output

Investments are the other major element in a bank's output mix. In terms of banking history in the United States, investment output, as represented by substantial security holdings, is a relatively recent development. During World War I security holdings by banks increased and continued to expand into the 1920s. A brief interruption occurred in this development during 1930-33 but thereafter the increase proceeded at an accelerated pace. Commercial bank investments increased and reached a peak of almost 100 billion dollars during World War II.

The investment output mix of commercial banks consists of various types of security holdings by banks. Corporate bonds, municipal securities, and government securities represent the principal holdings. Relatively unimportant to banks are corporate bonds. Increased construction of various public projects by municipalities and states following World War II has resulted in a marked rise in their borrowing. The satisfactory condition of local and state finances coupled with the increased vulnerability of commercial banks to federal income taxes and the tax-exempt features of local securities has resulted in a substantial holding of such securities by a commercial bank.

Holdings of U.S. government securities are an important item in commercial banking's investment output. During World War II the amount of these securities outstanding exceeded the amount that apparently could be readily absorbed by the nonbank public. Commercial banks with the aid of the Federal Reserve System, which provided them with sufficient reserves, absorbed the balance. Although banks continue to hold government securities, their importance in bank portfolios has tended to decline since 1951 following the "accord" between the Federal Reserve System and the Treasury.

PRICING OF INPUT AND OUTPUT

Pricing Input

Deposits are the most important raw material in the production of bank loans and investments. Commercial banks pay for these raw materials either through interest on time deposits or implicitly through remission of service charges on demand or checking deposits. Bankers have attempted to attract primary deposits in still other ways that do not involve direct payment for these raw materials. Architectural design of their banking establishments in the past has attempted to convey the solidity and solemnity of a Greek temple. In the postwar period, however, such design has given way to a more up to date approach, giving banking establishments a modernistic flair. There is also a tendency to replace or move out of public view the more "priestly" members of the banking fraternity and substitute in their place a "folksy" banker.

Banks have engaged in savings promotion campaigns such as the presentation of miniature vaults to the family offspring. Added services to the public such as drive-in banking and extension of services to the suburbs are additional cases in point. And in some areas, banks have served coffee to their morning customers. Additional examples of nonprice competition in banking are readily available.

To what do we owe these "forward" strides in banking? Perhaps the most important sponsor of nonprice competition for the raw materials of banking has been the Banking Act of 1933. Although this Act is considered by some an advancement in American monetary and banking thought, its sponsorship of nonprice competition and in banking leaves much to be desired. While ostensibly protecting the public against bank failures, the Act has almost frozen commercial banking into the mold of the 1930s. Under its sponsorship banks were prohibited from paying interest on demand deposits. Furthermore, limits on interest rate payments set by the board of governors on time deposits closed the route of escape for the banker whose preference may have been for price competition. Government intervention and enforcement was the logical outcome of earlier attempts by local clearing houses to set "standards" that smacked of monopoly. It is usually agreed that a monopoly worthy of the name cannot exist for very long unless the government's police powers are marshaled for its preservation. Attempts by clearing houses to impose on local bankers such standards as (1) maximum rates of interest to be paid in deposits; (2) banking hours and banking holidays; (3) prevention of multiple loans to customers; (4) uniform charges on services, were doomed to failure unless backed up with something more than threats.

In their attempts to set standards by reducing competition among its member clearing houses are similar to trade associations. A ready example is provided by the American Medical Association that has had a long and apparently unsuccessful battle with "witch doctors," "quacks," and "do it yourself remedies."[4] The Association achieved a measure of success when it obtained government support for its requirement that medical doctors be certified by members of its own fraternity — similar in effect to that required of plumbers by the local plumbers' union. That Scot surgeon and economist Adam Smith may not have been far off target when he warned almost two hundred years ago:

> People of the same trade seldom meet together, even for merriment and diversion but the conversation ends in a conspiracy against the public, or in some contrivance to raise prices.[5]

Pricing Output

Loans and investments are major elements in a bank's output mix and also its principal sources of revenue. Service charges on checking accounts and fees and commissions earned for services rendered customers are minor revenue sources. The bulk of a bank's revenues are, in effect, the product of the interest rate paid by its customers and the total volume of credit that a bank makes available.

Pricing of bank output by the banking industry differs in one important respect from practices usually followed by other industries in selling their products. The latter tend to confront their customers with established prices and terms of sales thereby permitting the exercise of consumer's choice. The banking industry, however, does not present its customers with established prices and other terms of sale. Each loan is individually negotiated between borrower and banker. Since each loan is likely to differ in its various details, the banker is apparently presented with a greater opportunity to exercise price discrimination than producers of other products.

A banker will take into consideration a number of factors in quoting a loan rate to a borrower.[6] For example, he will consider the financial size of the borrower or loan, the quality and type of credit, duration of loan, the nature and degree of risk, cost of administering the loan, competition among banks, the type of collateral, the borrower's average balances maintained at the bank, the importance of the account to the bank, and the character of the banker-customer relation. Perhaps the most important determinant of loan rates, however, is the availability of alternative sources of supply to the borrower. Borrowers with no alternative sources of supply for their credit needs are often at the mercy of the local bankers.

Scattered evidence seems to suggest that it is the relatively small or medium-size business that tends to pay a higher price for the banking industry's product. This may be attributed to the fact that a given size loan usually implies given conditions of risk, costs of administration of the loan, size of balances, and general worth to the bank. The net effect of these factors is that rates charged by banks tend to vary inversely with the size of loan. Since the loan requirements of small and medium-size businesses are relatively modest, their rates would be expected to be higher than those paid by large business enterprises. At the same time, a large business enterprise has many alternate sources of supply at its disposal. Such an opportunity is seldom available to a modest business concern. Governor Young summarized the extent of these opportunities in the 1930s in testimony before a congressional committee when many current restrictions were being imposed on banks.

> For instance, let us take a small community in South Dakota: A farmer who has to borrow $1,000 or $2,000 is known to the local banker and not known to anyone else. He cannot go to New York, Vermont or Maine and present his vote. No one knows him. Therefore, he has to pay the legal rate or contract rate . . . of, say 10 per cent. That is the rate he would probably have to pay to the local bank unless he was well enough known so he could go to a nearby town with a very desirable piece of paper and drive a bargain, say, for 8 per cent.[7]

If we take the statements of official banking spokesmen seriously, they indicate that the banking mentality at the time was dominated by the spirit of no price competition. Thus, one spokesman declared before a congressional committee:

> This competition between banks is in quality of service; . . . there is seldom a question of price; . . . there is no real problem of cheaper banking for us to solve.[8]

And another spokesman stated: "Banks have no bargains to offer, no cut rates."[9]

A number of other factors appear to be more important than alleged customer discrimination and nonprice competition in limiting the ability of commercial banks to service the needs of their principal customers — the small and medium-size business. Some of these factors are related to the nature of commercial banking and others to the pattern of public regulation that has restricted its operations.

In the past, bank lending has been conducted on the assumption that instability will tend to characterize the American economy. Accordingly, individual bankers will not assume ordinary risks if there is danger that the economy will be subject to sharp economic fluctuations. Moreover, selectivity of risks by banks is attributable to the fact that banks have a relatively small cushion of equity.

The short-term and unstable character of deposit liabilities force bankers to seek assets that will enable them to meet their liabilities under all foreseeable conditions. Even though bankers have an opportunity to borrow from the Federal Reserve System in the event of deposit withdrawal, they have concerned themselves, and according to some, excessively, about the composition and stability of their deposit liabilities. Tradition and concern lest such borrowing cast doubt on their credit position has made commercial banks averse to borrowing at the Federal Reserve System. And on this score the Federal Reserve System has done little to allay their fears.

Laws and administrative regulation are also factors limiting risk taking on the part of banks. Banks were not permitted to under-write security issues either directly or indirectly. They may not hold obligations of any one obliger in amounts exceeding a given percent of a bank's capital and surplus account. Moreover, examination of bank loan portfolios by government examiners has affected the readiness of commercial banks to make innovations in their business lending policies. And finally, usury laws have resulted in reluctance on the part of bankers to lend money at rates in excess of "standard" or "conventional" bank rates. One consequence is that some banks turned customers away rather than charge "excessive" rates while others evaded the law by employing service charges and other means to raise the gross interest rate. Much of this was to change, as we shall see, as banking moved through the 1960s, 1970s and into the 1980s.

CHANGING NATURE OF BANK LIABILITY MANAGEMENT

The behavior and activities of banks, especially large banks, has changed fundamentally since the 1960s.[10] They no longer accept deposits passively. Indeed through liability management they attempt to determine their own size. They now issue negotiable certificates of deposits (CDs), buy federal funds issue Eurodollars and foreign denominated liabilities, and issue subordinated debt. Their holding companies sell commercial paper and floating rate notes, and issue long-term debt. The proceeds from their various ventures are invested in a wide and complex array of activities, from domestic loans and investments to the large foreign loans discussed in this book. U.S. banks are interlocked with each other and with foreign banks through joint ventures and consortia. There thus seems to be no limit to the new markets and activities that U.S. banks will enter either directly or indirectly. The influence and power of banks, especially the large banks of the world, appears to give them an advantage in a seemingly endless variety of activities.

The rising aggressiveness of banks since the 1960s is consistent with the principle that competition is the best way to activate efficiency. Not everyone, however, agrees. They argue that banks' enterprising behavior makes the banking and financial system less secure, and monetary policy less effective, than if banks were more conservative in their behavior. The world debt fiasco, they note, is but one illustration of banks' rising aggressiveness.

It may be that the memories of loan losses and bank failures of the 1930s have now faded. It may be also that government monetary and fiscal policies since World War II have encouraged bankers to view another depression as unlikely. In either case bankers viewed loans as a more attractive alternative to their large prewar holdings of government securities and other conservative financial instruments. At the same time, as the pace of world economic activity accelerated and was reinforced by huge petro-dollars, so did the volume of domestic and foreign requests for bank loans. Most bankers chose to accommodate their customers' loan demands. They accepted reduced liquidity in exchange for higher profits.

They had an ample store of liquidity. In 1946 American banks' cash assets and U.S. government securities accounted for almost three quarters of their assets. By the end of the 1950s, however, bank lending capacity had largely been depleted. Although deposits had grown about 50 percent in the decade or so after the war, total bank loan volume level tripled. The loan-liquidity gap increased in the 1960s when corporations began to trim their demand deposits. Corporations no longer wished to hold large sums in interest-free checking deposits when they could use these excess funds to purchase interest-bearing Treasury bills and commercial paper.

Propelled by further loan growth and growing shortage of funds, banks went after new sources of liquidity. The large money center banks in New York and elsewhere began issuing negotiable certificates of deposit (CDs) at competitive interest rates. For all practical purposes these CDs were time deposits, and carried fixed maturity dates. The practice was encouraged by the development of a secondary market for CDs which in effect meant that these instruments could be sold before maturity if an invester needed his funds.

As a financial innovation the CD development was particularly successful. Banks learned that liquidity could be found on both sides of the balance sheet. Thus encouraged, banks could go to the money market either with their assets or liabilities for sale. This practice of issuing liabilities at competitive rates to fulfill cash needs is called "liability management". It is possible to combine asset liquidity with liability liquidity to support further loan growth.

In addition to the CD innovation, banks in the 1960s and 1970s began issuing other manageable liabilities. Federal funds trading, which had previously occurred in limited volume, grew rapidly. Banks borrowed Eurodollars from their foreign branches, and bank holding companies sold commercial paper and loaned the proceeds to their bank subsidiaries. The net effect has been that while almost none of the funds at large banks were derived from liability management in 1960 more than a third of such funds originated with such sources in 1983. It is the increasing reliance on liability management as a source of bank liquidity that is raising public concern.

Liability management, nevertheless, will continue and is very likely to increase as a result of the growing competitive environment of the banking industry. In comparison to regular deposit banking liability management is a more aggressive way to run a bank. As a result banks are more vulnerable to shifts in the financial and money markets. Since the practice is profitable for banks, they will continue it unless otherwise directed by markets and/or regulatory agencies.

Factors contributing to financial innovation are so important in changing the anatomy of banking and indeed the financial community in general. For this evidence I draw on William L. Silber who collected these innovations from articles cited in the *Wall Street Journal, Business Week, American Banker, Institutional Investors, Bank Marketing, Best's Review,* and other trade publications.[11] Most of these innovations can be attributed to economic incentives as we discussed. High nominal interest rates generated by inflation and regulatory constraint have provided the necessary incentives to encourage financial innovations. In general, banks and other financial institutions use financial innovations to reduce the constraints imposed upon them by regulatory agencies as well as economic forces. This is essentially the constraint-induced innovation hypothesis argued by William L. Silber.

Test results of this hypothesis are encouraging. For instance, Ben-Horin and Silber test the hypothesis by specifying a linear programming model of large money banks designed to calculate shadow prices of deposits and capital between 1952 and 1970. They report that shadow prices for deposits rose significantly in the years prior to 1961 and again before 1969. As we noted above, the 1960s were years of major financial innovation and indeed in 1961, the negotiable certificate of deposit came onto the scene, and in 1969 bank-related commercial paper and loan repurchases gained wide acceptance. Moreover, the shadow prices for capital in the Ben-Horin and Silber jumped significantly between 1962 and 1964. Again, in 1963 subordinated debentures were first introduced as part of bank capital, and in 1965 such debentures were issued in significant volume. In essence, rising costs of adhering to constraints encouraged financial innovation.

According to Silber's recent study, more than 60 percent of the innovations during the period 1970-82 are consistent with the constraint-induced model. Most of the balance can be attributed to technological changes and legislation factors. Moreover, both factors usually operate through constraints imposed on the bank or financial organizations, although both factors also have their own independent role in innovations.

Just as technological innovations improve economic welfare, so too financial innovations. They improve the ability of banks and other financial institutions to bear risk, lower transaction costs, and circumvent burdensome and outdated regulatory practices. They strengthen the ability of banks to serve the cluster roles which they play in our theory of cooperation.

NEW COMPETITIVE ENVIRONMENT

There is a feeling, some of it based on evidence, that not all banks can adjust to the new and highly competitive world of unregulated interest on deposits. Indeed in 1982 more than 42 bank failures are registered in the United States. Expectations are that the list of troubled American banks will grow. Regulators and Congress are showing a growing concern over these trends.

The net effect of the on-going shake-up in American banking nevertheless promises to have a major effect on the way financial services are delivered. As banks move aggressively into new lines of business and geographical regions they are also facing competition from businesses outside the traditional banking community. In March 1983, Citicorp, the second-largest bank holding company in the United States, broke the barrier between big U.S. commercial banks and the business of selling insurance when it agreed, in principle, to buy the American State Bank, Rapid City, South Dakota. A month later the First Interstate Bankcorp followed suit, buying Big Stone State Bank in Big Stone. Security Pacific Bancorp, too, has announced its intention to open a subsidiary in South Dakota where it expects to sell insurance.

All of this came about in March 1983 when South Dakota allowed bank holding companies to circumvent federal regulations by purchasing or establishing a state chartered subsidiary in the state through which they can sell insurance.

U.S. Congress in October 1982 had tried to restrict the insurance operation a bank may have. But it left a loophole by omitting any reference to state-chartered subsidiaries and that paved the way for the South Dakota law the banks have been seeking; now Delaware and Maine are working on similar bills.

Many observers believe that the banks' large customer bases and branch networks will enable them to offer a variety of insurance products at very competitive prices because of high volume and low start-up costs. That would be a boon to consumers but it would also force insurers to reduce their shrinking profit margins on such important insurance products as whole life and property/casualty insurance.

Other banks may follow if the remaining regulatory hurdles are cleared. Any state can prevent banks from selling insurance if its regulators determine that it would not be "fair and equitable" to the existing insurance companies and agents there. Furthermore, the Federal Reserve Board must also resolve whether insurance is a permissible "nonbanking" activity for banks.

Banks have also entered the brokerage business to establish a beachhead from which to move into other more profitable securities operations like underwriting and distributing new stock issues for corporations. At the same time banks are branching out, competition in financial services is coming from new areas. For instance, Sears Roebuck and Company is adding banks or savings-and-loan to its list which includes insurance, a real estate brokerage firm (Caldwell Banker), and Dean Witter, one of the nation's biggest brokerage firms. This enables Sears to boast of offering more financial services under the same roof than nearly anyone else can.

This change in the pattern of banking activity, moreover, has taken place without radical revisions in two key American banking laws. As we noted, the Glass-Steagall Act of 1933 separated the banking and brokerage business. Brokerage houses could not take deposits and banks could not underwrite or distribute new securities, although they could buy and sell stocks for customers. Until recently they were relatively minor players in the securities industry.

Moreover, at this writing Congress has not scrapped the McFadden Act, which confines banks to taking deposits in a single state. Their ability to move to other states has been accomplished under rapidly changing state law. Congressional committees, however, are gearing up for revisions of both major banking acts.

The regulatory system worked well enough until the roaring inflation of the 1970s made investors more interest-rate conscious. The birth of money-market mutual funds set off a fierce savings war between Main Street banks and Wall Street investment houses.

Driving the trend, as well, is an explosion in the use of electronic-funds-transfer systems. The effect has been to lower transactions costs in ways simply unforeseen by the legislation of the 1930s. Computers also can keep track of all of their customer's needs, opening vast potential markets for firms. For instance, an automatic teller machine could be used to place a stock order as well as to check a savings balance.

Despite such incentives, critics worry that the marketplace is getting too risky. Some question whether money-management conglomerates have the talent needed to successfully manage their diversified organizations. Others argue that mixing banking with general commerce could pose an even bigger threat. For instance, there is no sure way to insulate a conglomerate's banking subsidiary from economic difficulties experienced by nonbanking units.

On the other hand much of the opposition to changes in banking laws comes from people anxious to protect their own piece of the business. Several banks object to the economic power big banks can wield if allowed to move across state lines or merge with multi-national industrial corporations. Their fear is that such firms could have undue influence on legislators and even foreign governments.

There is little doubt that, stripped of pervasive regulatory support, the banking system in the years ahead will consolidate markedly in response to the demand and supply of financial services. Indeed, forecasts are for thousands rather than hundreds of bank and other financial service mergers in the next five years.

Some of the forecasts suggest that much of the activity will take place at middle-tier banks.[12] Small one-branch community banks will likely survive owing to their very strong relationships in the local markets. These markets are not large enough to attract major competitors. Large money-center banks are likely to remain strong competitors owing to economies of scale they can bring on lowering their costs of providing financial services.

It is, however, the middle-sized banks (those with assets of several hundred million dollars to several billion dollars) to decide whether to be predators or prey. They have relatively high cost structures, with 50, 60, or 70 branches. They are not as entrenched in their markets as small banks are in theirs and the markets where medium-sized banks operate are large enough to attract major competitors. Markets may also become more segmented whereby some banks will deal almost exclusively with the affluent customers, some will become more efficient business banks, and some will find efficient ways to serve the ordinary customer.

The concern with which bank regulators view the new found freedom of banks is suggested by moves at the federal level to put more discipline on the financial conglomerates.[13] At the same time the F.D.I.C. and other federal-insurance agencies propose a major revision of deposit-insurance rules to make bank managers, share-holders and big depositors assume some of the costs if a bank fails. As we discussed earlier, under the current system, federal agencies bear most of the costs when a bank fails. Under the F.D.I.C. plan, savers with no more than $100,000 would be fully protected, while people with larger deposits would not have full protection. Other measures aimed at slowing down the financial revolution include the comptroller of the currency moratorium until January 1, 1984 on so-called nonbanks — those operated by firms that are not in the regular banking business. The Federal Reserve has proposed that Congress ban temporarily acquisitions of banks and savings institutions by other firms until legislators can review the nation's banking and securities statutes.

Few people believe such action would more than slow the financial revolution. It is more likely that formal regulation will be supplemented with market discipline. In effect, investors and depositors will be provided with better information about financial institutions. Banks will be required, for instance, to disclose more about past-due loans, interest-rate sensitivities, and deposit maturity structures.

Another F.D.I.C. proposal would let state-chartered banks that it insures underwrite corporate securities. This is an important departure from the 50-year-old separation of the investment-banking industries. To be sure, the F.D.I.C. proposal includes several recommendations to insulate banks from the financial risks that might result from underwriting.

Under the proposal, banks could engage in underwriting only through subsidiaries. The subsidiaries would have to be physically separate from their affiliated banks and they cannot use the banks' names. It would also require three fairly conservative approaches to underwriting. One option would be to underwrite securities only on a *best efforts* basis — meaning the banks would try their best to sell the securities they underwrite but would not be required to purchase any unsold securities. Alternatively, banks could choose to confine their underwriting to highly rated securities. Or banks could limit their underwriting to shares in mutual funds that invest in short-term liquid assets.

The proposal would also limit the amount banks could lend both to companies whose securities they underwrite and to customers buying such securities. The restrictions are designed to prevent banks from taking loan risks to support their underwriting activities. Concerns about such potential conflicts of interest between underwriting and lending were a major reason for laws separating commercial and investment banking.

The Federal Reserve is strongly opposed to letting banks underwrite corporate securities. But if the F.D.I.C.'s interpretation of the law contained in its proposal is correct, the Fed would be powerless to prevent state-chartered banks, or non-Fed member banks from getting into the business. There are currently more than 9,000 such banks representing more than half of all U.S. commercial banks.

If the F.D.I.C. puts its plan into effect, national banks and other banks belonging to the Federal Reserve System might be tempted to switch charters so as to get into the underwriting business. If that happens it would be an uncanny repeat of history.

In years leading up the 1920s federal law prevented national banks from underwriting corporate securities. But many states did not impose such restrictions. In the 1920s many banks began switching to state charters to get into the securities business. To stem the decline in the number of national banks, the federal government dropped its restrictions in 1927. They were reimposed in 1933 after it was learned that some banks had run into trouble partly because of the free-wheeling dealings of their securities affiliates. By then, the 1929 stock market crash had damaged banks' enthusiasm for securities activities.

The vision of banking implicit in the current regulatory position is indeed broad. It includes the traditional banking services including commercial lending plus insurance, securities, real-estate, and savings and loan associations. In essence banks are now viewed as financial service enterprises though still separate from activities generally considered as commercial, for example, manufacturing or retail sales. The increased competitive environment will almost certainly strengthen the banking and financial role in the domestic as well as international economy. This can only be encouraged. In comparison to other industrial countries, however, American banking is still behind in many of its services to its customers.[14]

NOTES

1. See for instance, Leonard Lapidus et al., *State and Federal Regulations of Commercial Banks* (Washington: Federal Deposit Insurance Corporation, 1980) Vols. I and II; Albert Verheirstraeten (ed.), *Competition and Regulation in Financial Markets* (New York: St. Martin's Press, 1981); Almarin Phillips, "The Metamorphosis of Markets: Commercial and Investment Banking," *Journal of Corporate Law and Securities Regulation*, November 1978, pp. 227-43; F. R. Edwards (ed.), *Issues in Financial Regulation* (New York: McGraw-Hill, 1979); L. Golberg and L. White, *The Deregulation of the Banking and Securities*

Industries (Lexington, Mass.: Heath, 1979); J. Revell (ed.), *Competition and Regulation of Banks* (Cardiff: University of Wales Press, 1978); A. Phillips (ed.), *Promoting Competition in Regulated Markets* (Washington: Brookings Institution, 1975); Richard Dale, *Bank Supervision Around the World* (New York: Group of Thirty, 1982).

2. See, for example, George Macesich, *Commercial Banking and Regional Development in the U.S., 1950-60* (Tallahassee: Florida State University Press, 1965); M. A. Klein, "A Theory of the Banking Firm," *Journal of Money, Banking and Credit*, May 1971, pp. 205-18; J. J. Pringle, "A Theory of the Banking Firm," *Journal of Money, Credit and Banking*, May 1973, pp. 990-96.

3. In this chapter I shall adopt David Alhadeff's terminology and refer to deposits as the input of banks and loans and investments as their principal outputs. Such terminology is more accurately descriptive of the similarities among banks and other business enterprises in the private sector of the economy. See David A. Alhadeff, *Monopoly and Competition in Banking* (Berkeley: University of California Press, 1954); See also George Macesich, *Commercial Banking*, op. cit.

4. See the study by Milton Friedman and Simon Kuznets, *Income From Independent Practice* (New York: National Bureau of Economic Research, 1954).

5. Adam Smith, *Wealth of Nations* (New York: Modern Library, Inc., 1937), p. 128.

6. David A. Alhadeff, *Monopoly and Competition in Banking* (Berkeley: University of California Press, 1954), p. 112.

7. Hearings before the Committee on Banking and Currency, H.R. 71st Cong., 2nd Sess., *Branch, Chain and Group Banking*, Vol. I, p. 709. Also cited by Alhadeff, op. cit., p. 23.

8. Alhadeff, op. cit., p. 22.

9. Ibid., p. 22.

10. See, for instance, the various contributions in Thomas M. Havrilesky and John T. Boorman (eds.), *Current Perspective's in Banking: Operations, Management and Regulations* 2d ed. (Arlington Heights, Ill.: AHM Publishing, 1980).

11. William L. Silber, "Recent Structural Change in the Capital Markets: The Process of Financial Innovation," *The American Economic Review* May, 1983, pp. 89-95; Moshe Ben-Horim and William L. Silber, "Financial Innovation: H. Linein Programming Approach," *Journal of Banking and Finance* 1977, 1, pp. 277-96; William J. Silber, *Commercial Bank Liability Management* (Chicago: Association of Reserve City Bankers, 1978); see also Richard Sylla, "Monetary Innovations and Crises in American Economic History," in P. Wachtel (ed.), *Crises in the Economic and Financial Structure* (Lexington: D. C. Heath & Co., 1982); Albert Wojnilower, "The Central Role of Credit Crunches in Recent Financial History," *Brookings Papers in Economic Activity* 1980, pp. 277-36; Benjamin Friedman, "Postwar Changes in the American Financial Markets," in Martin Feldstein (ed.), *The American Economy in Transition* (Chicago: University of Chicago Press, 1980).

12. Tim Metz, "Medium-Sized Banks Are Told They Face Brunt of Major Drop in '83 Operating Net," *The Wall Street Journal*, May 9, 1983, p. 12.

13. For instance, Edward J. Kane ("Policy Implications of Structural Changes in Financial Markets," *The American Economic Review*, May, 1983, p. 100) writes ". . . Interest volatility and sovereign risk may be recognized as prime examples of risks that went largely unregulated in the recent past. Because unregulated risks are mispriced, insured institutions have an incentive to pursue them energetically. Failure to rationalize the pricing of Federal Deposit Insurance has interacted with technological change and interest volatility to increase the fragility of the entire financial system. The growing threat of worldwide financial crisis challenges regulators and politicians to find a way to price deposit insurance rationally. See also Edward J. Kane, "Accelerating Inflation, Technological Innovation and the Decreasing Effectiveness of Banking Regulation," *Journal of Finance*, May, 1981, pp. 355-67. See also John H. Kareken, "The First Step in Bank Deregulation: What About the FDIC?" *The American Economic Review* May, 1983, pp. 198-203.

14. According to one study, American banks, in terms of banking services offered, come in seventh in a group of ten industrial countries. The overall winner is Sweden, with Britain fourth and Italy at the bottom. "The Revolution in Retail Banking," *The Economist*, December 4, 1982, pp. 88-89.

6.

COMPARATIVE BANKING PRACTICES

BANKERS AND THEIR CLIENTS

Central bankers have pushed bankers to lend more to the debt-ridden developing countries while their governments push them into pet domestic projects including rescheduling of loans to important but troubled industries. In view of their recent experience bankers are naturally cautious. Not surprisingly this has had an understandable impact on their relations with their clients.

Changes are taking place as a result of foreign and domestic strains imposed on bankers. These strains resulting from issues originating in the international debt can be eased by the adoption of a Tit for Tat strategy as outlined in our theory of cooperation. How well are major international banks doing domestically? Here too the strains are evident.

To judge from a private survey of 99 international banks the institutions need to re-examine the manner in which they are dealing with the debt problems of large corporations.[1] The group of banks surveyed represents a cross section of the world's biggest banks. According to the survey, banks should commit more resources to debt restructurings. It also suggests that the institutions do not make enough of an effort to understand one another's attitudes toward a particular company's problems. Moreover, bank analysis of troubled loans are often superficial, and remedial action often unimaginative according to 87 of the banks polled.

According to all but six of the banks in the survey, banks leading restructurings often ignore hard realities. Indeed 89 banks say that at times the borrower is premitted to take the lead in shaping remedies. Senior bankers with restructuring experience willing to analyze a borrower's troubles are needed to make "rescues" work better. At the same time the survey finds that good lawyers and the ability to persuade banks with smaller loans to join the troubled company in the rescue plan are also important ingredients for success. Banks also view restructurings as time-consuming, costly, irregular, likely to lead to legal action, and a possibly thankless task.

The survey notes that conflict of interest often makes it difficult for banks to coordinate their approaches to corporate debt restructuring. Differences in the type and perceived quality of loans made by banks to the same corporate clients cause conflicts according to 86 of the banks in the survey. Thus, for example, one bank may have lent to a strong subsidiary of the company. Moreover, the loans may be secured in different ways. In addition, differences in the size and relative importance of the loans to banks and in the banks' willingness to advance new money to the borrower, are important causes of conflict in the view of 74 banks.

This chapter discusses the relationship between banks and their clients. In search for solutions to their financial problems, banks and their clients often fear that other countries are doing better. And indeed in some instances this is true. Though the various approaches and practices are not necessarily transferable, their study can be constructive. Given that the world's money and financial markets are highly interdependent, various approaches and practices however unique to a given country spill over and influence other countries. This is consistent with the strategy of Tit for Tat in our theory of cooperation.

COUNTRY PRACTICE

In Canada, for instance, the relationship between banker and client is very close indeed.[2] At times such a relationship presents a serious problem to bank and client. Consider the case of the Canadian Imperial Bank of Commerce (CIBC). It is Canada's second-largest bank and one which prides itself most on being banker to Canadian big business and Massey-Ferguson the world's biggest producer of tractors and the second-biggest producer of combine harvesters.

In Canada to be a main bank to a company is considered very important. It means that there are no rules restricting lending to any one customer to a certain percentage of capital. Unlike banks elsewhere it is thus not forced to parcel out or syndicate big loans among competitors. As a result a company's main bank is very much involved with the company.

What this means is illustrated in *The Economist*.

> . . . CIBC's loans to Massey-Ferguson amount to C$340M, excluding the C$100M which the bank wrote off when the near-bankrupt tractor maker was bailed out by its creditors and the Canadian government in 1981. CIBC's loans to Massey-Ferguson are three to four times the size of those from any other Canadian bank. . . . Another of CIBC's troubled domestic customers, Dome Petroleum borrowed an amount equal to more than half the bank's equity — a figure looked on with horror south of the 49th parallel.[3]

When a series of setbacks overtook Massey-Ferguson beginning for the most part in 1978, CIBC was left with a large bad debt, a desire to spread the risk of large corporate clients more widely and a determination to monitor more closely its customers in the corporate sector.

The Economist is certainly correct on the need to monitor when it writes that

> . . . most economists agree . . . that companies are the engine of growth in every country. Companies create the wealth which governments and individuals consume. And yet, in most economies, it is the corporate sector which is the least analysed and least understood. . . . Failure to monitor properly or even to publish (let alone analyse), data on companies' financial health has had disastrous consequences. Chronic financial mismanagement has gone unnoticed. Company liquidations everywhere are approaching the levels of the 1930's and, in OECD countries alone, 32M people are unemployed. . . .[4]

The fast pace of inflation during the decades of the 1960s and 1970s has led firms to rely increasingly on shorter-term borrowing and average maturity of the debt has decreased sharply. At the same time, firms have sold off their short-term financial assets so that their liquidity ratios, that is, financial assets divided by short-term liabilities, have also worsened. These ratios fluctuate with the business cycle deteriorating at the outset of the cycle and improving toward the end.

The tendency over recent cycles, however, has been that these ratios are not being restored to the precycle values. There appears a general deterioration in the values over the several postwar cycles. Their restoration, according to some observers, requires massive corporate bank and equity issues. For instance, in the early 1950s American corporations' short-term debt was a little more than a third of their long-term debt. In 1982 it was almost 100 percent. Furthermore, the long-term debt of 20 to 30 year bonds is increasingly replaced by five to ten year loans and notes. For the same years, the ratios of American corporations' liquid assets to their short-term market debt has fallen from two to less than half.

According to the New York firm of Solomon Brothers whose 1982 report on the financial deterioration of American corporations makes a case for such deterioration also discusses the notion that inflation and increased borrowings are good for business. That is to say, by borrowing to finance acquisitions of real producing assets whose value appreciates while the liability depreciates is simply not correct. It is not necessarily good for business as is often implied. The report underscores that in 1949 the up-to-date valuation of net worth of American nonfinancial business was $2.02 for each dollar of debt. By the end of the 1970s the ratio was $1.36. In short, as inflation and borrowing have accelerated, equity prices have lagged. The supposed higher return to share-holders has not materialized for the reason that the value that the market has put on each increment of current-cost net worth brought about by new borrowing has not occurred as rapidly.

A similar situation also appears to exist in other industrial countries. Drawing on the June, 1982 quarterly report of the Bank of England, *The Economist* observes that average debt-equity ratios for British industrial and commercial companies were at a 16-year low in 1981.[5] To judge from another unpublished study by the Bank of England, the experience of British companies mirrors that of the American. One important difference is that the real return on capital employed dropped further and faster between the early 1960s and 1981, when it hit a low of 3 percent in Britain, than in any other major industrial country.

Italy with accelerating inflation and higher debt-equity ratios than in Britain has significantly increased debt-servicing costs. In a 1981 study by Mediobanca which is the country's long-term lender, high interest ratios are reported as responsible for restricting many of the country's companies from undertaking long overdue modernization and expansion programs. The results of the study indicate that in private-sector companies about 70 percent of the preinterest profits go to interest charges.

In France available corporate data are sketchy. Such scattered evidence as exists suggest that French companies' need for external financing is considerably greater than in Britain, Germany, or the United States. Internal funds as a proportion of spending on fixed assets and stocks were only 51 percent in France in 1981 compared with 80 percent in Germany, 88 percent in the United States and 108 percent in Britain.[6]

In Germany concern with the long-term deterioration in the industrial capital base is underscored by a Bundesbank report in November 1982 citing a modest rise in companies' equity (or own funds) of only 3 percent. Thus in 1981, equity accounted for only 20.5 percent of the balance sheet total compared with 21 percent in 1980, 26.5 percent in 1970, and roughly 30 percent in 1965.

The Bundesbank, according to *The Economist*, is aware of the reasons for the decline including at the top of its list the insufficient earning power of the enterprises. This in turn has prevented firms from generating adequate internal funds. Potential investors are hesitant to provide risk capital. Firms as a result were pushed to resort to increase borrowing leading to additional interest payments and thus to a further reduction in earnings.

By Japanese standards the country's firms appear to be doing well in terms of financing. Thus the Bank of Japan reports that the corporate sector's demand for external finance has dropped. In 1974 it was 11.3 percent of gross domestic product. On the other hand OECD estimates for July 1982 show the ratio of liquid assets to current liabilities slipping to 0.28 in 1980 and 1981. This would appear to be about the same as for the United States. These figures however, are not strictly comparable.

Nevertheless, the estimates do suggest that in the countries under review there is a pronounced deterioation in the corporate sector of the economy. To judge from estimates quoted in the Salomon firm study, more than $10 billion a month in 1983 in the United States alone will be required to restore the corporate debt-maturity ratios even to the levels of the early 1970s. According to *The Economist* the monthly average in 1983 is estimated to be about $3 billion, significantly below the figures reported as required by the Salomon firm if the American corporate sector is to reverse its secular decline.

The deterioration of the industrial capital base in many countries has prompted banks to evaluate their relationship with many of their past best customers. To judge from evidence reported by the top 20 American regional banks for 1982 they were taking off 0.73 percent of their average loans outstanding of earnings on the assumption that they would now be repaid. This is worse than the 0.56 percent reached in 1976. These are for domestic customers and do not include the more dubious foreign loans.

The changing relationship between banks and their corporate customers is also suggested by the prevalence in America of disintermediation or short-cutting the banking system. Thus corporations no longer turn to banks for short-term credit. They now issue commercial paper which is picked up by the money market funds. The amount of such paper in the United States doubled between the end of 1979 and the middle of 1982.

On the other hand, the decreased credit rating of many corporations has also pushed their paper out of the money market funds and back to bank borrowing. At the same time banks offer to back up lines of credit to many companies in the event that their access to the market is closed.

In any case the changing relationship reinforced by borrowers shifting to commercial paper forced banks to look elsewhere. Flush with OPEC deposits in the 1970s, banks were forced to do something with these deposits if returns were to be earned. Some found an outlet for profitable loans in corporations too small to issue their own commercial paper. This was indeed lucrative for banks so engaged since they could charge at prime rate or above to these firms without worry that their loan offers would be turned down. This is the development of the so-called *middle market* in the United States facilitated by the increasing scope of nationwide banking.

Competition in the middle market, however, has reduced banking profits thanks to the entry of many more banks into the market. In addition, the smaller corporations themselves began to understand better their own improved bargaining position which resulted in many receiving loans at the prime rate or even below.

As a result of the growing indebtedness of American corporations the role of bank lending has also changed. In many corporations it is now increasingly long-term rather than short-term cyclical finance provided by commercial paper. Indeed, banks are being tied more closely to their corporate customers as a result. Banks now find it difficult to shed one of their clients however desirable it may be for the bank. Nonetheless, banks have also learned as a result that they must be actively involved in a corporate crisis if they are to influence the outcome.

In financially sophisticated Britain critics charge that banks have not invested enough in industry. What they did lend was short-term and not enough. Banks claim that while they are prepared to lend for a longer period, they can not force on their clients fixed term loans. Industry has apparently a preference for the flexibility of an overdraft typically used in Britain.

Moreover, British banks do not wish to become major equity holders in the businesses of their clients. In fact, it is because they avoided becoming shareholders, so the argument goes, that British banking is characterized by stability which it presumably would not have. There are, however, some notable exceptions where banks have stepped in and converted loans into preference shares.

British banks do support their clients and sometimes with the assistance of the Bank of England. This is usually the case where several banks are involved in a troubled company. The Bank of England assumes a coordinating role for the banks' efforts at rescue.

Indeed, the Bank of England, unlike most central banks, has always been a bank and manages to keep a hand, so to speak, in a few commercial accounts so as to keep in touch with the world outside of central banking. Its involvement as coordinator in industrial rescue operations, however, goes beyond this. It has always acted as a sort of semi-official go between. Unlike in the United States, rescue operations are not guided by banks, nor by the central government as in France and Germany nor by law as in Italy, but rather by the Bank of England.

This role for the Bank of England is explained by the absence in British companies of any one lead bank as in Germany and France and many small banks as in the United States. The cooperation and coordination is thus made simpler between the Bank of England and the big London clearing banks. Observers have remarked that it would indeed be ironic if the British system of coordination and reserve operations would lead to more industrial rescues and for longer.[7] After all, the Bank of England is also the supervisor of banks and responsible for ensuring that they are not reckless in their operation.

On the continent the German universal system of banking maintains a durable and interlocking relationship with the country's industries. This arrangement has been suggested by many observers in the past as a model for other countries. Not even Germany and its universal banking system has been spared dealing with serious problems since the country's economy became stalled in the late 1970s and early 1980s. The German banking system is in fact, more deeply committed and involved with whatever industrial rescue operations may be required than is true of banks in other countries. There is, moreover, little they can expect in the way of support from government.

Such an arrangement has permitted German banks to swap debt for equity during the 1930s while in the United States the Glass-Stegal Act prohibits such activities. This is but an illustration of the considerable power exercised by German banks. This has led in turn, to conflicts of interest on more than one occasion. Some banks, for instance, have become so entangled with the affairs of their clients that they may be at the same time its client's biggest creditor and principal shareholder.

Various German commissions, however, viewed the possibility of conflict of interest as not a significant problem with universal banking. Thus the Gessler commission in the late 1970s recommended that banks should merely draw up a code of good conduct. A more restrictive recommendation was that banks should be limited to 25 percent plus one share in their holdings of industrial equities. There is, moreover, a problem of selling off the large pieces of industrial equities that banks hold without disrupting the economy. Owing to its limitations, the German stock market provides little help in this direction.

One reason for the relative underdevelopment of the German stock market may well be that bankers make a better profit by lending than by issuing stocks and bonds. This is also suggested by the capital base of German industry in terms of the decline of its own funds in its total balance from 27 percent to 20 percent over the last decade. Indeed there has not been a major bond issue in Germany during the entire decade of the 1970s. How long German banks will be able to support financially such troublesome heavy industry giants as well is an open question. Inability on their part may well drive a government wedge between them and their clients as some observers believe.[8]

It is said that in France wherever money moves, the bank of the centralist government can be found directing it. This is understandable. The country's three largest commercial banks have been nationalized since 1946. Neither right-wing nor socialist governments in France see any reason why they should not be nationalized and with the arrival of the socialists in 1981 the remaining banks, except the 150 or so foreign banks, were nationalized. Thus the idea of government intervention into the country's economy is not a monopoly of any single political party.

All big French companies have a so-called *lead bank*, which is the company's biggest creditor. It is one of the responsibilities of the lead bank to file with the French central bank every one of the company's credit facilities over $3.7 million (FFR 25 million). The lead bank is, in effect, also in charge of the six to 12 banks that typically constitute a company's principal creditors.

If problems develop with one of its clients, the lead bank takes up the case with *CIRI* (the Comité Interministériel de Reconstruction de l'Industrie) which in effect is charged with dealing with the country's financially sick companies. The organization is as mysterious and forbidding as the Paris Club which, as noted elsewhere, is an informal group of Western government creditors to the heavily indebted developing countries. Some indeed have described it as a "black box".[9] It is composed of representatives from several French ministries and a secretariat whose members search out and discuss a company's problems with bankers, unions, and suppliers to determine a course of action to be recommended to the CIRI and by it to the government.

There are a number of obvious problems connected with CIRI. For instance, what does it do when confronted with a sick private company that is in competition with a nationalized one? What does CIRI do when domestic buyers for a company cannot be found but it is reluctant to sell to a foreigner? What role do foreign banks have in the bailouts? Can government really make decisions on only economic and not social grounds? Since bankers and industrialists in the country take orders from ministries and not the market, can CIRI be sure that all wisdom lies within the ministries?

Italian industry's dependence on banks is well known. So too is the large number of banks (1,080 in 1982) serving the country's industries. A medium-sized company commonly deals with 20 to 30 banks, a big one deals with 40 to 50. The country's system of credit ceilings which is the governments only control over the money supply also encourages a company in dealing with many banks. Thus if any one bank is close to its credit ceiling the company can readily turn to another.

In effect, Italian companies are heavily dependent on the short-term lending of their bankers. This in turn makes them highly sensitive to interest rates. They cannot readily move into a longer-term market since loans over 18 months are in the hands of special long-term lending institutions which must issue bonds in competition with the government and its huge deficit amounting to almost 17 percent of the gross domestic product in 1982.

When an Italian company is in trouble there is no lead or house bank to which it can turn. It turns to the laws for help. For such help it can call on four important laws passed during the difficult financial period of the 1970s. Thus LAW 675 is the government's safety net and the only restructuring law that allows direct contributions from the state. LAW 787 was designed specifically to restructure the country's troubled chemical industry. LAW 95 is most widely used and permits a court judgment to freeze a troubled company's debts for two to three years with a moratorium on interest-rate payments. New loans can be authorized by court decree and thus can be made eligible for government guarantees. Indeed, it is expected that these laws may be extended to include so-called healthy companies if it can be shown that financial restructuring would help them to be more competitive internationally.

Elsewhere on the continent significant differences also exist. In particular, Yugoslavia provides a unique combination of socialist and market elements in its banking organization which merits a closer examination.[10]

"Basic banks" represent the core of the country's banking system. They perform the main part of financial intermediation.

They are "mixed" banks, engaged in all bank operations: short-term and long-term; domestic and foreign; with socialist and private subjects. They are primarily funded by Organizations of Associated Labor or OAL's by self-management agreement and represent their "associations" in performing services in financing.

An important consequence of such management is that basic banks are not profit-oriented institutions. They are primarily designed to provide for their members the maximum of financial resources at the minimum cost. In addition to OAL's members, basic banks may be internal banks of OAL's (similar to the finance department of companies), self-management communities and other socialist institutions, excluding governments.

Organization of basic banks differs in important respects from profit-motivated banks elsewhere. Thus the top management body of the bank is the assembly, comprising representatives of all members of the bank with equal voting power. The assembly elects the executive board responsible for the implementation of its decisions and guidelines. It also appoints the manager of the bank responsible for the efficient working of the bank and implementation of decisions taken by the assembly and by the executive board. The assembly also elects credit committees which decide on individual credit applications, within the framework of credit policy designed by the assembly and the executive board. Finally, the supervision board, elected by the assembly, is responsible for the legal conformity of bank operations. The bank's staff has its own management bodies, responsible for decision making on employment and dismissal of personnel, incomes (within the framework decided by the assembly), and working conditions. The highest management body is the assembly of workers' community, which elects the workers' council and committees responsible for the various activities. These workers' management bodies, however, do not decide on bank policy.

Although banks are not profit oriented, there is a net income. These banks usually have three funds, reserve fund, joint liability fund, and business fund. The reserve fund is designed for securing bank liquidity. Therefore, resources of this fund are held on account with the central banking system. The joint liability fund is aimed at covering losses resulting from uncollectable claims. The business fund provides for resources for fixed assets of the bank (premises, equipment, and so on). In addition to these funds, bank solvency is guaranteed by its members by their total assets (unlimited guarantee).

In addition to these mandatory funds, banks may have other funds, as decided by the assembly.

Basic banks represent financial institutions which are, on the one hand, very similar to banks in developed market economies and on the other hand also rather different from these banks. They are similar in their operations to banks in developed market economies. They are different in respect to their motive. They are not profit minded. Their operations are primarily motivated by the needs for financing on the part of their members who are at the same time their main borrowers. This results in motivation for maximizing the amount of credit availability and minimizing the cost of credit at the same time. Also, their operations are significantly determined by their share in financing of priority needs listed in the social plans, and accepted by banks by signing self-management agreements.

Next in importance in the country's unique financial structure are associated banks. They are established only by basic banks. Legislation leaves considerable freedom for banks to transfer various types of their operations to these associated banks, or to use them as their agents for all types of domestic and foreign transactions, excluding operations in sight deposits and operations with individuals. In practice foreign exchange operations are the main operations of these banks. In this way, associated banks represent institutions which significantly contribute to the integration of the banking system, although thus far mainly within territories of individual republics and autonomous provinces.

Both basic banks and associated banks are obliged to implement monetary measures decided on by the central banking system. The central banking system supervises bank liquidity and prescribes measures for improvement of the liquidity of individual banks. It decides on penalties if these measures are not followed and initiates the judiciary procedure against such banks and their management.

Basic and associated banks are allowed to perform foreign transactions only if they fulfill a list of conditions assuring that the bank is able to perform these operations successfully. So far (1983), 21 banks have permission to perform foreign operations. In case a bank fails to settle its foreign obligation by the date of maturity, the National Bank of Yugoslavia may settle the obligation and then order the Social Accounting Service (which handles the giro account of the bank) to charge its account for the dinar counterpart of the obligation paid on behalf of the bank, in favor of the National Bank of Yugoslavia.

To American and European observers Japanese industrial finance is too debt-heavy and bank dependent. This may have been adequate during a time when banks and industries had a unity of purpose. It may no longer be true.

Most Japanese companies have a main bank similar to the lead bank in France and the house bank in Germany. The importance of the main bank to a company depends on which of the three predominant corporate structures it belongs to. In the family-controlled Zaibatsus, for example, Mitsubishi, Sumimoto, and similar groups along with manufacturing, trading, and other companies can be found a commercial bank. The banks are simply part of the entity without a dominant influence on the group's activities.

In groups such as Sanwa and Dai-Ichi Kangyo the bank tends to be more dominant and the interlinking of the group's companies weakest. The units are more independent financially than in the traditional Zaibatsus.

The third group focuses around such manufacturing entities as Toyota. The group's trading company acts as a banker to the large number of small suppliers in such groups. Ties with any given commercial bank are not as close.

The Japanese system is, in effect, geared to commercial decision making so that bankers do not play as important roles as in Germany. There are no proxy votes, and little actual power is in the hands of bankers. The power structure is tilted to the production rather than financial or banking side of business.

This does not mean that Japanese bankers are without power. They do have power and they exercise it. Although commercial and investment banking is legally separated as in the United States, securities firms have charged that interference by bankers in industry's affairs has been a key reason why companies have tried to reduce their dependence on bank finance. Indeed, increasingly big Japanese companies are going directly to the open market as a source of external funds.

Resort to the capital markets for external financing by Japanese companies, however, is far from easy. Only the largest and best companies can pass the severe tests imposed on entry into these markets. It is charged, moreover, that banks are strongly opposed to any loosening of their requirements which would permit more entries into the market. Banks have good reason to resist on no changes since the share of bank borrowings in the total of small and medium-sized companies has never been below 90 percent since 1972.

In times of troubles, however, a company can turn to its lead or main bank for more than solace and advice. It can count on its bank to act as a rallying point or a catalyst for a solution. There is seldom talk of receivership or liquidation. Sometimes the solutions include not only financial assistance but the actual loan of employees from other firms. Consensus and unity of purpose is standard Japanese practice for troubled companies. This practice also serves well for viable new projects and companies. Indeed, it is from such arrangements that ventures in high technology have come.

There is reason to believe that this may be changing as a result of Japanese companies becoming increasingly less dependent on their banks. Companies appear to be relying more on internal financing as well as making greater use of the market for their external requirement through independent security dealers. There is also the entry of foreign banks into the Japanese financial markets. Their entry promises to increase competition which may eventually entice major Japanese companies from their main banks. There is also the growth of joint industrial ventures in the country, which has cast up the issue of divided loyalties to the banks of several companies.

The net result appears to be dissolution of the once strong ties between Japanese banks and industries – a process underway all over the world. Thanks to its consensus decision-making tradition, Japan may not be overwhelmed by the process.

Outside the United States, Europe, and Japan, Hong-Kong and Singapore have the greatest concentration of banks and financial institutions. On occasion their sophistication exceeds that of London and New York. They have prospered because of convenience to the Asian mainland and islands by providing financial services including laundering money from such illegal activities as drugs and piracy. An educated labor force, many with English language skills, in Hong-Kong and Singapore serve them well in meeting the requirements of international finance. All these factors are further reinforced by the inability of other Asian countries to put together a banking and financial organization capable of transferring capital from the industrialized countries and Middle East to the rapidly developing countries of East Asia.

For their part, Singapore specializes in collecting and trading money. Hong-Kong specializes in the syndication of loans to Asia because of closer connections to New York and London as well as tax advantages. These activities complement one another. This may be changing as the two Asian centers are competing for each others' business. This is understandable in view of the importance of financial services to national income in both. Indeed Singapore employs 7.6 percent of its labor force in financial services while Hong-Kong with a labor force twice the size employs 5 percent.

Neither Singapore nor Hong-Kong has a central bank. Self regulation of financial institutions is apparently taken seriously in both city-states. In Singapore, for instance, a proposed merger of the Monetary Authority of Singapore, which supervised banks, and the Board of Commissions of Currency, which is the city-state's note issuer, for the purpose of establishing a central bank, was never carried through. Hong-Kong has undertaken what some observers view as a vain attempt to control domestic inflation by taking its banks more firmly in hand.

In Hong-Kong attempts to set interest rates through an informal cartel of banks was, in effect, subverted by the activities of newly established wholesale banks called deposit-taking companies. These companies increased their loans by more than 60 percent in 1981-82 while bank loans increased by less than 30 percent. At the same time the deposit-taking companies undercut the semi-official interest rates. This may change since the authorities are attempting to make the cartel a statutory body. It is a good guess that banks owning these companies will surely figure a way to evade and/or avoid the efforts of the cartel and authorities to restrict their activities.

The development of an increasingly sophisticated capital market in the two city-states has also increased competition by commercial banks, investment banks and stock firms. These organizations are now offering their clients an extensive list of services outside their traditional business. Indeed, business is so good that banks and brokerage firms outside the region are moving in to take advantage of its growth.

CHANGING PERCEPTIONS OF BANKERS

How have the changes we have discussed affected bankers? This is difficult to say. It is simply difficult to gauge the full effect of these changes on bankers carrying out their day-to-day business. A number of observations, however, can be made. One is that bankers are becoming more risk conscious if not indeed risk averse. They are taking a very close look indeed into the books of their present and prospective clients with the idea of lending less for shorter periods rather than more for longer periods.

Second, they are attempting to charge a market price for each of the services they offer, no longer are they as willing as before to cross-subsidize some services to their clients.

Third, banks are carefully watching their exposure to various sectors of their countries' economies. Most banks have always considered themselves better able to judge the domestic economic situation than the foreign scene. This has been amply demonstrated in the years since 1979. There is also an awareness on their part that by supporting ailing companies in a given sector they have made the situation difficult for healthy companies. Thus there is now a tendency to restrict bank exposure to the whole sector irrespective of the merits of an individual firm.

Fourth, bankers now feel there is a limit to the extent they can support any given sector or industry of the economy. Indeed only banks, government, and employees typically can make financial concessions to keep afloat a sinking company. Wage cuts by employees of problem companies in the United States are now common. Bankers would like to see the same practice extended to other countries as well.

Fifth, there is concern about adequacy of bank capital. Essentially the foundation on which a bank rests, capital is defined by regulators as stockholders' equity, together with such items as loan-loss reserves and debt convertible into stock. Regulators use capital to gauge the loan and securities losses a bank can absorb before sliding into insolvency.

Capital, of course, is not an infallible guide to banking strength. More than 9,000 American banks failed in the 1930s even though their capital ratio was 13 percent. In 1980 the average capital ratio at the 17 big American multinational banks had deteriorated to 4.6 percent from 5.1 percent in 1977. In December 1981 the comptroller and the Federal Reserve Board decreed that all but a few banks should maintain capital ratios of at least 5 percent.

The banks excluded were the big multinationals. Their existing capital ratios would have made a similar requirement unrealistic.

They were given a year or two to come up to requirements. This appears to be a manageable problem.

It is the implication of the new minimum capital requirements that are worrisome to banks. For instance, each $100 million in bank capital permits lending of up to $2.2 billion at a $4.5 percent capital ratio, but an increase of half a percentage point in capital means lending must be $222 million less.[11] According to some estimates it was largely by maintaining lower capital ratios that big banks could generate annual loan growth of 12.7 percent over the period 1979-82. A higher capital ratio may slow down loan growth. It may also force banks to be more insistent that a loan provide a solid return and repayment prospects.

It is clear that the new capital rule will have important effects on the on-going merger and consolidation in American banking. Quite simply banks wishing to merge and buy other banks will need regulatory approval. To do so they must show the authorities a very good capital position to gain approval. There is also the fear held by some bankers that the new capital ratio requirement will be used to slow down the flow of credit to the economy if traditional methods prove ineffective.

Finally, experience with industrial bailouts has brought about a closer tie between banks and industry. Their interest in seeing to it that a firm is profitable has brought this closer tie. It has also increased bank expertise in various industries. On the other hand, there is a detectable drift in that for many banks and firms the desire for long-term growth has given way to the need for short term survival. This is unfortunate indeed for future growth in many countries. On the other hand, the problems themselves are also bringing about a new era of cooperation between bankers and their clients which may very well overcome many of these difficulties.

The short-term effects of the changing perceptions of bankers is suggested by a decline in net bank lending abroad. Thus, while the level of loan commitments in the first quarter of 1983, totalling $19.3 billion, was only slightly below that in the same quarter of 1982, about $9.4 billion of the total was extended to Brazil and Mexico. These sums according to the IMF report, accounted for about 80 percent of new commitments to nonoil developing countries.[12] The otherwise substantial pace of decline in new loan commitments, especially to nonoil developing countries, reflected the preference of international banks for curtailing medium term syndicated sovereign lending in favor of project-related and trade-related finance and loans organized through private placements.

NOTES

1. Peter Truell, "Money Banks Concede Their Own Failings in Restructuring Firms' Debt, Study Says," *The Wall Street Journal*, May 20, 1983, p. 35. The study referred to is by Professor Charles Williams, Harvard Business School and commissioned by international banks. The 99 banks answering the survey have considerable experience with large corporate debt problems: 71 have significant loans to International Harvester Co.; 63 to Chrysler Corp.; 39 to Mexico's Group Industrial Alta S.A.; 36 to Massey-Ferguson Ltd.; and 20 to Dome Petroleum Ltd.

2. In addition to *The Economist*, March 26, 1983, this chapter draws on E. I. Altman and A. W. Sametz (eds.), *Financial Crisis: Institutions and Markets in a Fragile Environment* (New York: Wiley-Interscience, 1978); J. Revell (ed.), *Competition and Regulation of Banks* (Cardiff: University of Wales Press, 1978); U.S. Congress, House Subcommittee on Financial Institutions, Supervision, Regulation and Insurance of the Committee on Banking, Currency and Housing, *Financial Institutions and the Nation's Economy* (FINE) *Discussion Principles* (Hearings, 94th Congress, 1st and 2nd sessions, December, 1975); A. Verheirstraeten (ed.), *Competition and Regulation in Financial Markets* (New York: St. Martin's Press, 1981); Interbank Research Organization (ed.), *The Regulation of Banks in the Member States of the EEC* (Alphen/Rijn: Sijthoff and Noordhoff, 1978); A. P. Jacquemin and H. W. Jong, *European Industrial Organization* (London: Macmillan, 1977); J. E. Wadsworth, J. S. G. Wilson, and H. Fournier (eds.), *The Development of Financial Institutions in Europe, 1956-1976* (Leyden: Sijthoff, 1977); A. S. Courakis (ed.), *Inflation, Depression and Economic Policy in the West* (London-Oxford: Mansell Publishing-Alexandrine Press, 1979); George Macesich, *Money in a European Common Market* (Baden-Baden: Nomos Verlagsgesellschaft, 1972); G. Carli (ed.), *La Struttura del Sistema Creditizio Italiano* (Bologna: Il Mulino, 1978); F. T. Blackaby (ed.), *British Economic Policy, 1960-1974* (Cambridge: Cambridge University Press, for the National Institute of Economic and Social Research, 1978).

3. *The Economist*, op. cit., pp. 14-15.

4. Ibid., p. 20.

5. Ibid.

6. Ibid.

7. Ibid.

8. Ibid.

9. Ibid., p. 56.

10. See Dimitrije Dimitrijević and George Macesich, *Money and Finance in Contemporary Yugoslavia* (New York: Praeger Publishers, 1973); Dimitrije

Dimitrijević and George Macesich, *Money and Finance in Yugoslavia: A Comparative Analysis* (New York: Praeger Publishers, 1984); Rikard Lang, George Macesich, and Dragomir Vojnić (eds.), *Political Economy of Yugoslavia Since 1974* (Zagreb: Informator, 1982).

11. *Business Week* July 18, 1983, pp. 148-49.

12. International Monetary Fund, *Survey* August 22, 1983, pp. 252-53.

7.

MONETARY FINANCIAL ORGANIZATION IN DEVELOPING DEBTOR COUNTRIES

THE ISSUE

The prospects for future bank lending will depend more on the willingness of the world banking system to intermediate internationally in the face of heightened risk perceptions and concerns about capital adequacy rather than on its ability to do so.[1] The message to developing debtor countries is clear. If they are to participate fully in the tournament they must show world banks that in fact they are viable players who will cooperate and not defect. Among other things this can be done by strengthening the ability of their monetary and financial organizations to marshal domestic savings and allocate these resources effectively and efficiently. These prospects are, of course, important to our theory of cooperation based on reciprocity. This chapter examines the experience of several of the countries.

FINANCIAL INSTITUTIONS AND ECONOMIC DEVELOPMENT

As we noted, net new international bank lending declined sharply in 1982 for the first time since 1977, owing to heightened perceptions of risk in international lending, concerns about prudent bank practices, and the effect of the world economic recession.[2] More important to the developing-debtor countries is that the slow down

129

has been accompanied by shifts in the composition of borrowers. The share of net new bank lending going to the nonoil developing countries declined in 1982. In the first quarter of 1983 total new bank lending commitments, particularly to nonoil developing countries, declined substantially. Furthermore there is a preference on the part of international banks for curtailing medium-term syndicated sovereign lending in favor of project-related and trade-related finance organized through private placements.

It is imperative that developing debtor countries turn to reconstructing and or developing monetary and financial institutions capable of marshaling and allocating domestic savings if they are to develop. Each country, of course, is constrained by its own culture and familiarity with what it already has. But, within the constraints, the different experiences of others can be constructive.[3]

Historical data on most countries support the view that economic growth and development are closely associated with the growth and development of financial institutions.[4]

The growth of an economy requires the proper allocation of resources to their most efficient uses. Resources flow from households to producers offering the highest relative price for their services. It is only with the use of money that these allocations can properly and effectively be carried out. While production is made possible by the use of money, the distribution of real income to the various segments of the economy is also accomplished with the use of money.

Though it may be possible to accomplish the task of allocation, utilization, and distribution of resources without money, the mechanism will not be as smooth as with the use of money when a society becomes more complex. The growing complexity of society requires the use of money on a very wide scale. This complexity introduces the exchange relation between one country and the rest of the world. It involves international trade with imports and exports becoming very essential to the economic life of society. This in turn requires a deepening of the use of money internally as well as externally.

Money and its concomitant financial institutions have developed gradually over a long period of time. Money in its many forms has been with us for a long time; and it has taken many forms before the present one, which cannot be regarded as final. The functions of money may be classified into two broad categories: static and dynamic. By its static function, money serves as a passive technical device ensuring a better operation of the economic system without actively influencing its trends. By its dynamic function money tends to exert a powerful influence on the trends of the price level, on the volume of production, trade, and consumption, and on the distribution of wealth. It is capable of stifling or stimulating economic and social progress.

One important question, then, is how does an economy become highly monetized? An answer is provided by examining the facilitating financial institutions and agencies that made the monetizing of an economy possible within a relatively short period of time. Such financial institutions and agencies are the following:

Commercial banks and their availability on a large scale;
Cooperative activities of commercial banks as agents of modern economy;
The existence and dynamic role of a central bank and its influence on the activities of commercial banks in providing credit;
Establishment of agricultural credit and industrial development banks;
Role of government in such activity as regulating financial institutions, providing minting operations, taxing and revenue collecting, and disbursing activities.

DEMAND AND SUPPLY OF FINANCIAL INSTITUTIONS

One approach to the development of financial institutions places emphasis on the demand side for financial services. It is argued that as the economy grows it generates additional new demands for these services, which bring about a supply response in the growth of the financial system. Accordingly, the lack of financial institutions in a country is simply a lack of demand for their services. This approach, or "demand-following" approach as it is sometimes called, implies that finance is essentially passive and permissive. Various historical examples may be cited in support of this approach. Late eighteenth- and nineteenth-century England can be cited as an example. Undoubtedly strong barriers exist at times to an increased supply of financial services in response to demand. Ready examples are provided by the restrictive banking legislation in nineteenth-century

France and religious barriers against loans and interest charges. Another example is provided by the abortive upswing of Italian industrial development in the 1880s, mainly because the modern investment bank had not yet been established in Italy. Other examples will be found in this study in the case of U.S. banking and the restrictive influence of outmoded ideas in the theory of money and banking. In effect, the lack of financial services inhibits effective growth patterns and processes.

Another approach emphasizes the supply side or, as it is sometimes called, the *supply-leading* phenomenon. In essence, this approach places emphasis on the creation of financial institutions and the supply of their financial assets, liabilities, and related financial services in advance of the demand for them. The supply-leading approach concentrates on the transfer of resources from traditional sectors to the modern growth sectors and on the promotion and stimulation of activity in the modern sectors. Financial intermediation that transfers resources from traditional sectors, whether by collecting wealth and saving from those sectors in exchange for its deposits and other financial liabilities, or by credit creation and forced saving, is akin to the concept of *innovation financing*. The use of the *demand-leading* approach is a more moderate form of financial development. Its use may in fact slow economic development. It will tend to discriminate against smaller industries and borrowers. It lends itself, moreover, to the development of monopoly trade.

The supply-leading approach may be used to encourage and stimulate rapid economic development by increasing monetization of the economy. It may aid economic development and planning by channeling investible funds to certain agreed-upon priority sectors.

MONEY MARKET

There is no standardized universally accepted definition of the term *money market*. In its broadest sense, the money market denotes all the available facilities for borrowing and lending money. In this sense the money market excludes the market for long-term funds as the *capital market* and restricts the term money market to the market for short-term funds. It is in this narrow sense that money market will be used in this study.

For an individual banker the money market provides a place where changing liquidity requirements can be accommodated; but it is much more than that. It also serves the liquidity needs of an endless variety of individuals, business, and government units, foreign as well as domestic. It is an invaluable agency for promoting the flexibility, mobility, and full utilization of a country's resources. In addition, it is the principal point of contact for actions of the central bank designed to improve the operation of the economic system.

The existence of a money market implies two essential conditions. The first is a significant volume of highly liquid assets, which in effect means assets that can be exchanged for cash quickly and without substantial loss. The second requirement is a relatively high degree of concentration, geographically speaking, in dealing in these assets. The market may and ordinarily does serve an extensive hinterland; and it is likely to have connections with other money markets. The transactions themselves, however, focus in a limited area.

In the more highly developed money markets a common characteristic is a wide variety of liquid assets, possessing different features and serving different purposes. A corresponding variety and degree of specialization is to be found among the organizations and affiliated businesses dealing in these assets. The result is likely to be a more efficient market as indicated by services performed, economy of operation, and uniformity of charges. Major money markets such as New York, London, and Paris have close connections with one another as well as with local money markets within their respective countries. They are closely integrated also with their central banks, which tend to assume the role of ultimate guarantor of liquidity or lender of last resort.

Accordingly, we may look on modern money markets as centers where highly liquid assets are bought and sold. This observation gives the key to what they are and to the basic functions they perform. It also provides the key to the institutional structure of the money market. The organization of the money market can be described in terms of three types of participants: suppliers and demanders of liquid assets, providers of ancillary services of a specialized character, and suppliers of routine mechanical services.

Suppliers and demanders of liquid assets are combined into one category, because the same participant may appear as supplier

at one time and demander at another. There are, of course, exceptions to this statement. Nevertheless, it is useful to view the institutional aspects of the money market in terms of demand and supply
for liquid assets. We may indicate briefly by way of illustration the
major suppliers and demanders of funds in the New York money
market:

	Suppliers	Demanders
Commercial banks	XX	X
Dealers and brokers		XX
Other financial corporations:		
Life insurance companies	X	
Finance companies		XX
Domestic business corporations	X	XX
Exporters and importers		XX
Foreign banks and others	XX	
Government		
Federal		XX
State and Local	X	X
Federal reserve banks	XX	

The XX indicates a major role and X a minor role. The listings are
not in order of importance in terms of volume. For example, the
federal government is by far the largest demander of short-term
funds. We have indicated whether a particular agency or business is
to be regarded as supplier, demander, or both. Commercial banks
are considered primarily as suppliers of short-term credit. In the
United States the so-called money market banks include the larger
banks in New York City, a half-dozen in Chicago, plus perhaps 20
or so scattered throughout the country. The exact number included
in this category varies inasmuch as shifts in prevailing money market
conditions tend to make banks sometimes more and sometimes less
money market conscious. Thus the number may rise when credit continues tight for some time and decline when it eases. By means of
correspondent relations with the large city banks, the temporarily idle
funds of a great number of small banks scattered all over the country
are brought within the orbit of the New York money market. By the

same token funds may move away from New York to the more local money markets under the attraction of yield differentials.

Of course, at the same time that some banks are supplying funds to the money market other banks may well be there as demanders of liquid assets. Thus, for example, a bank may borrow federal funds or sell Treasury or other types of assets for cash in order to replenish its reserves.

Another major category of participants in the money market consists of dealers and brokers. They require money for the purpose of carrying inventories of securities during the period when these are being distributed to the public. Government securities dealers are specialists who in fact make a market for government securities by continuously buying and selling all maturities. Of perhaps the most important dealers engaged in this business, five are banks (three in New York and two in Chicago). The role of dealers and brokers then is twofold: They are an important source of demand for short-term financing, and they themselves constitute a part of the market mechanism.

Life insurance companies are primarily suppliers of long-term funds and for that reason are more likely to participate in the capital market. At times they may also offer funds on a short-term basis while awaiting opportunity to dispose of such funds on a long-term basis.

Finance companies utilize large sums of money in connection with installment sales and personal loans. Since they find it necessary to supplement their own funds, their finance paper is offered on the market in substantial amounts.

Domestic business corporations have become important suppliers as well as demanders for short-term funds. Prior to the early 1950s there was little incentive for corporations to invest their idle funds on a short-term basis owing to the low rates that prevailed in the money market. This has changed thanks to the rise in interest rates and growth in financial innovations. Many corporations now are quite alert in placing idle funds to work in the money market as we have discussed elsewhere.

Exporters and importers have now achieved the prominence in the New York money market that they have in London, for example. Moreover, the development of other types of credit instruments in place of the trade acceptance often sent along with a bill of lading further decreased the importance of exporters and importers.

The post-World War II period witnessed a significant upsurge in the volume of short-term funds invested in the New York money market by foreign banks, international institutions, and a considerable part can be attributed to the expansion in the resources of the IMF with the resulting increase in its holding in the United States.

The U.S. government, however, constitutes by far the largest net demander of short-term funds in the money market instrument in the post-World War II period and has played a significant role in this development. The Treasury bill market involves a continual turnover of maturing bills and their replacement with a new series.

The money market is entered from time to time by state and local governments in order to meet various requirements prior to receipt of tax revenues. The instrument typically used is the *tax anticipation note*. They may also enter the market as suppliers of short-term funds by placing their excess cash funds in the market.

The major current and contingent supplier of funds to the money market, however, is the Federal Reserve Bank. The importance of Federal Reserve (central bank) credit operations to the money market is very significant indeed.

Suppliers of mechanical services to the money market include such routine services as telephone, telegraph, transfer, safekeeping, maintenance of records, and printing. Mechanical and routine as they are, they are nonetheless very important and help to explain in part the concentration of money market activities in particular localities. Such concentration results in economies whose effects are to lower the costs of conducting the operations of the money market.

The specialized services are those in such fields as statistical bureaus, credit-evaluating organizations, and securities analysis groups. These services also tend to be concentrated in large cities, partly because of the advantages of obtaining the latest detailed information by being on the scene. The New York Clearing House and similar institutions in other cities provide both mechanical services and information to the money markets of which they are a part. Previously, Federal Reserve System clearinghouses provided emergency liquidity in periods of credit stringency by pooling resources and issuing highly negotiable certificates that at times even circulated as currency.

As in any market, the money market is a place where prices are determined. These prices establish the level and structure of short-term credit instruments.

A linkage exists within the structure of rates so that a major influence affecting one of the rates is likely to be felt all along the line. This means that the entire complex of interest rates tends to move more or less together, though the degree of movement may vary substantially, particularly over short periods of time.

The similar movement of interest rates may be attributed to several factors. Thus factors affecting one type of credit are likely also to influence others. There is, moreover, a high degree of substitutability among different types of credit instruments. The net effect is that any substantial distortion in the pattern of yields among the different types of credit may be expected to set forces in motion that will tend to correct the distortion.

The linkage of rates is, moreover, spatial in that a connection exists between rates in different parts of the country (and between countries) and among scattered money markets. Internal and international shifts in short-term funds occur if they are not prevented from doing so by various controls.

Indeed these linkages fairly well measure how developed and mature a money market is. In developed money market adjustments within the structure of rates and in relationship of rates throughout the economy, changes constantly will take place. However, they will take place rapidly and smoothly. For these reasons I would argue that in the United States and in some European countries, a developed and mature money market exists and in others it does not as we shall see in the case of developing-debtor countries.

Treasury bills and federal funds provide a nearly perfect medium for adjusting the liquidity needs of commercial banks and in fact of the entire business community. Such other securities as banker's acceptance commercial paper and finance company paper contribute to the same end. Holders of idle funds can turn to the money market and there find instant employment for such funds. In effect, it is the money market that principally performs the function of facilitating the adjustment of liquidity requirements. The principal instruments for doing so are federal funds and Treasury bills as well as many of the new instruments we discussed earlier.

In essence, the money market facilitates the management of earning assets. By contributing to the liquidity of assets held by the banking system it helps increase the amount of liquidity available to the entire economy.

SOCIOECONOMIC, LEGAL, AND POLITICAL SYSTEMS AND FINANCIAL INSTITUTIONS

Those familiar with problems of comparative monetary and financial analysis are also aware of the influence a country's economic, legal, political, and social system has on the roles that money and financial institutions play. The role of money in an economy, and therefore the importance of monetary policies and institutions, depends upon the power of monetary decisions in the spending and saving decisions of households, firms, and the public or government sector to influence those real processes by which income and wealth are created and distributed. In all modern, contemporary economies this power of money to influence real processes is limited by the scope of direct administrative controls, whether they are exercised by individual decision units or by some other local or central authority. In contemporary economies these decisions concerning the real processes are implemented by some combination of monetary and administrative means.

It is necessary to distinguish between the degree of control central authorities in a country may have and the specific balance between monetary incentives and administrative controls by which these authorities need to implement their decisions. The evidence suggests that the degree of reliance that central authorities place on administrative measures as opposed to general monetary measures has tended to increase with the degree of centralized control over economic activity. Theoretically, of course, this need not be the case. Monetary incentives need not be replaced by direct administrative controls as the degree of centralization of economic decision increases. Thus central authorities with complete control over wages, prices, and the financial system, including the state budget, can so design the structure of money incentives and obligations as to force firms and households to produce any final bundle of goods and services within the productive capacity of the country's economy. The required degree of sophistication and precision on the part of monetary and financial institutions to achieve these results, however, is simply not available to any contemporary economy.

Few countries have elected to copy faithfully any given monetary model. In every case the monetary and financial organization is related to and has grown out of the distinctive economic, legal, political, and social traditions and the objective economic conditions of its specific environment. The Yugoslav case is an excellent illustration. Yugoslavia attempted to imitate the Soviet monetary and financial model, then, disillusioned with that, a mixed Soviet-Western model. What actually resulted is a model that in many respects is uniquely Yugoslav, consonant with other Yugoslav institutions and traditions. Another illustration is provided by the Kemmerer missions in the 1920s and their imposition of inappropriate and irrelevant central banks on countries of Latin America.

GENERAL CHARACTERISTICS OF FINANCIAL INSTITUTIONS IN SELECTED DEVELOPING COUNTRIES

Our theory tells us that transformation of savings into investment is facilitated by allowing interest rates to reflect actual market conditions. They do not always do so. In good part governments use the interest rates and other prices as a tool in their attempts to stimulate economic growth. Such manipulation of prices is not very successful to judge from the record.

In its sixth World Development Report the World Bank examines the way developing countries control prices including interest rates, exchange rates, wages, as well as many others.[5] In one sample of developing countries the World Bank finds that prices in the 1970s were controlled least in Malawi, most in Ghana, with a wide range in between. The bank used its index of price distortions to estimate what each country's growth rate was, and then compared that with what actually happened. The evidence in Figure 7.1 suggests the discrepancy between estimates and reality. It shows that growth depends on many things (for example, resources, political stability) apart from price distortion. Nevertheless, price distortion could explain about one-third of the variation in growth among countries. As the bank succinctly puts it, "prices do matter for growth."

The more far-sighted governments should and do take such evidence seriously. They understand that it is entrepreneurial skill and human capital rather than politicians and bureaucrats that are the mainsprings of development. Moreover, it is extremely difficult

FIGURE 7.1

Distortions of Prices, 1970-80 (*Average of the effects of foreign exchange pricing, factor and product pricing).

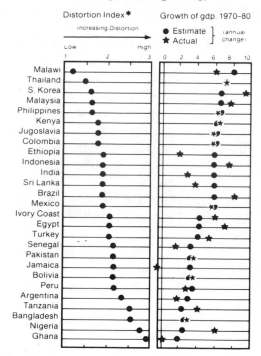

Source: World Bank and *The Economist* (July 30, 1983): 61.

to dismantle official controls over the direction of credit and investment once they are established.

Even so, no developed country has found that merely establishing the appropriate financial framework — proper supervision, prudent lending, ensuring the absence of fraud and so on — is the end of its task. For instance, governments will not allow foreign banks to establish themselves within domestic banking systems and give them free rein there. Few local banks, so the argument goes, would be able to compete. Every country feels the need for a home-grown financial sector, because of the central role banks play in economic and monetary policy.

Most developing countries share another characteristic. They all fail to cast the commercial banking net wide enough. Small craftsmen, artisans, and especially farmers who typically comprise between 50 and 80 percent of the total labor force rely on family, friends, or money lenders for credit. Such lending institutions as the government typically favor larger economic units. Subsidized credit, moreover, means rationing the amount available which is usually at the expense of smaller operators.

They also share a lack of confidence in financial institutions, which results in weak banks, and weakening confidence in proper assets, generally making it difficult for a long-term capital market to develop. Gold holdings in many of these countries underscore the lack of confidence in financial institutions. Several of these countries need to widen their financial markets to get more people to hold bank money. They also need to deepen their capital markets so that institutions can give better service to individual companies' financial needs.

Taiwan and South Korea are examples where capital markets under strong government influence and control may well have outgrown their financial organizations. These countries have attempted to pattern their financial sectors on the Japanese model of a decade or so ago. Interest rates were kept artificially low and investment steered into leading export industries. Indeed, until recently three out of five big banks in Korea were owned by the government. In Taiwan all but three banks are owned by the government.

In both countries the financial system tends to freeze out small businesses. These businesses turn to the unorganized markets for loans usually at very high interest rates. The opportunities for fraud and abuse in some of these "unofficial markets" are well known. In Korea, for instance, where businesses provide IOUs to their lenders, a recent practice has been to demand more IOUs from their debtors and then sell them. When people started to present their IOUs some of the companies which had borrowed the money collapsed.

In Japan small business has access to regional banks for loans. It is thus not crowded out now though Japan gave considerable help to favored industries. Nominal interest rates, moreover, were kept low in the 1960s in good part because inflation was low. The country's experience, nevertheless, does serve as an important model to Taiwan and South Korea as to what they can expect as they continue to develop.

Indonesia, Thailand, and Philippines are important sovereign borrowers whose performance over the decades of the 1960s and

1970s is nonetheless much better than most countries in Latin America and Africa. They have grown much faster with less inflation than most Latin American and African countries. They have done it with a less sophisticated financial system than their Asian neighbors.

Thus the growth of the banking system in Thailand reflects the country's economy which grew by 6 percent in 1970-75 and by 8 percent in 1975-79. Banks expanded rapidly in the rural areas, encouraged by the Bank of Thailand. Indeed commercial banks borrowed heavily abroad to meet rapidly growing domestic demand for credit. Their net foreign liabilities rose from $200 million in the early 1970s to more than $1.5 billion in 1979.[6] Foreign borrowing is encouraged by strict usury laws. These laws prevent interest rates from rising and thus discourage domestic saving to match the increase in investment thereby encouraging foreign borrowing. In Thailand, moreover, matters are not helped by government efforts to force banks to lend to farmers whose default record is very high.

A more sophisticated financial system than in Thailand is in place in the Philippines. It is the method of doing business, including banking, in the Philippines which leaves the outsiders perplexed. Very simply it is business and banking by the clan. It is similar in nature to the Japanese *zaibatsu*. Such an arrangement of family-owned conglomerates can frustrate government policy designed to encourage efficiency in industry and banking.

In fact, out of 28 commercial banks in the country 23 belong to ten family groupings which dominate the economy. According to one study these groupings are made up of interlocking directorships drawn from about 90 families.[7]

The typical Filipino banker is not really in the banking business per se. He uses his bank for allied business.[8] It is not altogether surprising that the country has had more bank failures than any country in the region.

In the Islamic Republic of Pakistan an attempt has been underway since 1981 to have banks offer interest-free financial instruments along with conventional loans and deposits. The motivation is the Koran's injunction against *riba*, which means interest in Arabic. This is a significant departure from conventional banking practices.

Thus, debt of all kinds is eliminated under Pakistan's experiment. Instead, banks supply financing as equity or investments. According to the government view, a Western banker does not take the same risk as the borrower. As a result the conventional loan is not "equal" and thus is not Islamic. Needless to say, Pakistan is having considerable difficulty in promoting its Islamic concept of banking. Critics doubt that bankers who are used to lending with limited liability, will suddenly know enough about all businesses to make wise investments.

There is, moreover, Pakistan's borrowing from Western lenders, such as the World Bank, that do charge interest. Someone has to pay those charges, and in practice the Pakistan government still passes them on to private borrowers. It even collects a commission as the middleman.

Matters are not much better in Latin America. Indeed, in Peru, the country's sixth largest bank, Banco Commercial, almost collapsed thanks to its president and chief executive who lent $60 million of the bank's money to his own business ventures to buy 56 percent of the bank. About $20 million of their loans will have to be written off as bad debts.[9]

In Venezuela we have the case of BTV (Banco de los Trabajadores de Venezuela), the country's largest bank and its failure. The central bank claims that many of BTV's $6 billion worth of loans have been lent unsecured and on a personal basis.

In Chile estimates indicate that 6 percent of all bank loans are in effect bad. One bank, Banco de Chile, is suggested to have as high as 30 percent of its loans in this category. Matters are not helped by the fact that shares of Banco de Chile have been used as collateral for foreign loans.

In Yugoslavia, the case of the Zagrebačka Privredna Banka, one of the country's largest banks, moved dangerously close to insolvency in 1982 as a consequence of bad loans. It was rescued at the last minute thanks to efforts on the part of the country's entire banking community.

In a cross-comparison with other types of economies, the structure of financial institutions in Yugoslavia suggests the greatest similarity with the market developing economies, and with good reason. Similarity in decentralized decision making and the role of financial institutions in financial intermediation and monetary developments under these circumstances on the one hand, and the relatively low per capita income on the other result in the dominant role of deposit banks, nearly all of them being monetary institutions, both in Yugoslavia and in the market-developing economies as well. However, the process of decentralization of economic decision making in Yugoslavia, and the resulting decrease in the role of semi-financial intermediaries and in specialized banks deviates from the relatively important role of these institutions in other developing economies. Finally, the role of institutions financed on the market (*banques d'affaires*, industrial banks, etc.), insurance institutions, unit and investment trusts, and investment companies, the stock and bond market[10] is rather small in these countries, if it exists at all.

In comparison with developed market economies, the basic difference is the lack of the last above-mentioned group of financial institutions. Thus, the structure of financial institutions in Yugoslavia appears far less differentiated than in the case of developed market economies, particularly with respect to institutions working on financial markets.

The greatest difference appears in comparison to the structure of financial institutions in Yugoslavia with those in socialist central economic decision-making economies. In these economies, the structure of financial institutions usually involves only the central bank, and some specialized government banks, particularly for foreign transactions. This is logical under conditions of central economic decision on production prices (saving investment, where autonomous financial intermediation is not significant and monetary developments have a different role in comparison with that in economies with decentralized economic decision making).

In this way, the degree of decentralization in economic decision making, as one of the basic components of the economic system, appears as the main determinant of the structure of financial institutions. The level of economic development is also significant, but less than the economic decision making.

The specific feature of the Yugoslav economic system is reflected also in significant specific characteristics of the share of individual types of financial institutions in total assets-liabilities of these institutions. Using Goldsmith's presentation of "Distribution of Assets of Financial Institutions,"[11] the share of the central banking system in total assets of financial institutions is more similar to that of developed (.17 percent in 1981) than that of developing economies. However, it may be useful to mention that the development of the percentage share of the central banking system in total assets of financial institutions started in the case of Yugoslavia from nearly 100 percent, and in the case of developed economies from 0 percent, or nearly 0 percent in the case of developing economies.

The second specific characteristic is the high share of deposit banks, but rather low share of thrift institutions in total assets and liabilities in the case of Yugoslavia, compared with developing market economies, and particularly with developed economies. Thus, the share of deposit banks in total assets of financial institutions in Yugoslavia amounted to 80 percent in 1981, compared with 44 percent in the case of developing economies and 29 percent in the case of developed economies according to the above-mentioned Goldsmith's table. At the same time, the respective percentage share of thrift and insurance institutions was less than 1 percent in the case of Yugoslavia, compared with 18 percent in market-developing economies and 42 percent in market-developed economies.

For their part, the International Monetary Fund and the World Bank are urging universal, general purpose banking in the place of specialized financial institutions. Securities markets are no longer considered particularly important. Subsidies are out. The focus now is on dismantling government policies that thwart financial development.

The Fund can play a very constructive part in promoting a more efficient monetary-financial organization in developing-debtor countries. It already encourages increased domestic savings and use of market rates of interest in countries seeking IMF assistance. As a condition for such assistance the Fund can also insist that developing debtor countries reconstruct and/or establish more effective and efficient financial organizations.

International banks can also play a similar role. Our earlier illustration of Citibank and Chase Manhattan Bank's operation of a subsidiary Banco Lar bank in Brazil are but a case in point.[12] Apart from obvious difficulties with local currency lending, these banks can fill existing gaps in the financial organizations in these countries. For instance, when the Brazilian government told banks they could open two offices in the hinterland for each one they closed in the established banking center of Rio and São Paulo, U.S. banks quickly moved into locations such as Riberirao Preto, the sugar growing capital, and São Luis, the new shipping port serving the mineral-rich Carajas region. According to Citibank it moved into Belém and Manaus in order to obtain a larger portion of the country's internal cash flow. With 12 branches Citibank is competing with Banco Lar's 42 branch network and Banco de Boston's five offices to offer customers collection services. Brazilians use banks for payments of rent, tax, and utility bills to creditors.

Such arrangements, however, are not always enthusiastically received by host governments. Thus *Business Week* reports,

> Many foreign bankers are angered . . . that Brazil keeps milking them for dollar loans, yet refuses to allow them majority positions in local operations. 'Why is it that only Chase, the Bank of Boston, and Citi can operate branches in Brazil and not us?' Complains a U.S. banker. The answer may be that the price is too stiff. The senior vice-president of one major U.S. bank was recently told that 'for $50 million he could get into Brazil.' The payoff was termed 'a gift to the government.' The bank backed off.[13]

Mexico in turn is restructuring its banking system, which was nationalized in 1982, by merging small banks into larger ones and by eliminating some small credit institutions. This will leave Mexico with 29 credit societies compared with 60 banks and credit institutions at the time the banks were nationalized.

The reorganization leaves 17 banks intact and merges 20 smaller institutions into 12 large banks. Eleven small credit institutions will be eliminated entirely. Mexico is still working out the compensation for most of the former owners. The first round of compensations was carried out by issuing bonds to the former owners of 11 banks. The maximum limit for payment in full is set at 10 years.

The banks will be operated according to government policy to aid the country's economic development. In the interest of efficiency, banks will be required to compete. The industries formally belonging to banks are to be sold off. They will not be integrated into the state sector but kept separate.

This illustrates the nature of the problem. It is difficult enough for an individual, without a spiritual revolution, to change his or her character. It is even harder for millions of individuals to change their system of social values.

The frustration of being able to change neither the nature of the challenge nor one's own ability to meet the challenge is compounded when this frustration is imposed on the citizens of a young, unself-confident newly independent state. They have the humiliation of seeing some of the economic assets of their country owned or run by foreign nationals. They loathe the foreigners but cannot do without them. The solution, too often, is to remove the threat by driving it out.

This shortsighted view demonstrates well a decision to "defect" rather than "cooperate" in our iterated Prisoner's Dilemma game. By adopting a strategy of cooperation, both the developing-debtor country citizens and developed country bankers would gain. As we noted, the real costs may be in the tertiary effects when the debtor country's defection turns into self-punishment. This is seldom taken into account by decisions to defect. The consequences may be monumental.

NOTES

1. *International Capital Markets: Developments and Prospects 1983*, Fund Occasional Paper No. 23 prepared by R. C. Williams and P. M. Keller (Washington: International Monetary Fund, 1983).

2. Ibid., pp. 252-53.

3. See George Macesich and H. Tsai, *Money in Economic Systems* (New York: Praeger, 1982); George Macesich, *The International Monetary Economy and The Third World* (New York: Praeger Publishers, 1981).

4. The following studies provide useful insights into the role of money and monetary and financial institutions in development. R. Goldsmith, *Financial Structure and Development* (New Haven. Yale University Press, 1969); R. I. McKinnon, *Money in Economic Development* (Washington: The Brookings Institution, 1973); E. S. Shaw, *Financial Developing in Economic Development* (Oxford: Oxford University Press, 1973); Peter Drake, *Money, Finance and Development* (New York: Wiley, Halsted Press, 1980); G. Horwich and P. A. Samuelson (eds.), *Trade, Stability and Macroeconomics* (New York: Academic Press, 1974); M. G. Hadjimichacakis, "Equilibrium and Disequilibrium Growth with Money – The Tobin Models," *Review of Economic Studies* October, 1971, pp. 457-79; F. H. Hahn, "On Money and Growth," *Journal of Money Credit and Banking*, May 1969, pp. 172-84; B. K. Kapur, "Money as a Medium of Exchange and Monetary Growth in an Underdevelopment Context," *Journal of Development Studies*, March 1975, pp. 33-48; D. Levhari and D. Patinkin, "The Role of Money in a Simple Grants Model," *American Economic Review*, September 1968, pp. 713-53; W. A. Lewis, "Economic Development with Unlimited Supplies of Labor," *Manchester School of Economic and Social Studies*, May 1954, pp. 131-91; K. Nagatani, "A Monetary Growth Model with Variable Employment," *Journal of Money, Credit and Banking* May 1968, pp. 188-206; H. Rose, "Unemployment in a Theory of Growth," *International Economics Review* September 1966, pp. 260-82; M. Sidrauski, "Inflation and Economic Growth," *Journal of Political Economy* December 1967, pp. 796-810; J. J. Seigel, "Inflation, Bank Profits and Government Seniorage," *American Economic Review* Papers and Proceedings, May 1981, pp. 352-55; J. J. Stein, "Monetary Growth Theory in Respective," *American Economic Review* March

1970, pp. 85-106; J. Tobin, "Money and Economic Growth," *Econometrics* October 1965, pp. 671-84; R. C. Kumar, "Money in Development: A Monetary Growth Model à la McKinnon," *Southern Economic Journal* July 1983, pp. 18-36.

5. World Bank, *World Development Report* (Washington World Bank, 1983). See also, *The Economist*, July 30, 1983, p. 61.

6. *The Economist* November 13, 1982, p. 16.

7. Ibid., p. 21.

8. Ibid.

9. *The Economist* December 18, 1982, p. 84.

10. According to the classification and information in *Capital Markets Study, General Report* (Paris: Organization for Economic Cooperation and Development, 1967), p. 152. See also Dimitrije Dimitrijević and George Macesich, *Money and Finance in Yugoslavia: A Comparative Analysis* (New York: Praeger Publishers, 1984).

11. Raymond W. Goldsmith, *Financial Structure and Development* (New Haven: Yale University Press, 1969), Table 5-23, p. 267.

12. "How Foreign Banks Still Get Rich in Brazil," *Business Week* August 22, 1983, p. 102.

13. Ibid.

8.

THEORY OF COOPERATION AND MONETARY STABILITY

DEBT DEFAULT ISSUE

According to some accounts the Dutch Republic would have been a contender for leadership in the Industrial Revolution if the Dutch had kept their loanable funds at home instead of squandering their savings through loans to the Amsterdam money market to pay for wars, the court extravagances, and the bureaucratic corruption of the despots of Europe.[1] The Napoleonic Wars, subsequent inflation, and default eroded the Dutch capital stock. The Dutch banking community never regained its prewar position. Indeed, the Amsterdam money market was but another casualty of defaulted international loans. Contemporary talk of a "debtors' cartel" — a combine of countries that would call for a debt moratorium — may be the prelude to massive international debt default.[2]

    Indeed, the subject of default has generated considerable interest.[3] Default is an option which developing-debtor countries can exercise. The term *default* here is used to refer in a general sense to any alteration of a financial contract between a domestic debtor and a nonresident creditor. It is a time-inconsistent policy similar to such a domestic policy as a monetary policy rule for a given growth in the money stock as argued for by Monetarists and discussed elsewhere in this book. Such a monetary policy rule is an agreement between the government and the public. Governments can and do violate such a monetary policy contract if they feel other more important goals can be achieved by doing so. For instance, government may manipulate the money stock in violation of the policy contract in order to take advantage of the short-term nonneutrality of money for purposes of temporarily reducing unemployment. Such a scenario has been performed and played out by governments of some developed-creditor countries prior to national elections with some success.[4]

Naturally such violations reduce the usefulness of future monetary policy contracts. They do, however, have an immediate distributional income effect between debtors and creditors. Their long-term effects are more difficult to quantify although the credibility of the government and its monetary authorities are cast in doubt. Subsequent monetary manipulation will likely prove unsuccessful and counterproductive.

Similarly the exercise of a default option by government may occur when a country's aggregate income is unusually low so that not all claims on it can be satisfied. It may then feel that more can be gained by, in effect, rewriting the existing assortment of contracts. The government thus becomes a sort of arbiter that allocates the country's short-fall in aggregate income among competing groups — domestic and foreign. This is an important role for government and its exercise may be crucial. Without effective arbitration the attempt by one group to exercise its individual rights may force other groups into bankruptcy or revolution. The resulting decline in asset values imposes more costs on all parties without dealing with the issue of allocating the smaller aggregate income. The alternative to default thus may be very large political and economic losses, which could be more disruptive for the country than default.

One can hope that governments under the circumstances would choose a collection of defaults on domestic and foreign contracts, which would minimize the damage and long term interests of both domestic constituents and foreign debtors. Since the foreign debtor is not directly represented in the political process, he is more vulnerable. There is thus an incentive for the foreign creditor to strengthen his claims through the insured financial intermediaries of a third country whose government is influential in the political processes of the debtor country. Moreover, in the insured financial sector of the third country the costs of a given failure can be spread to taxpayers of the third country.

All of this haunts contemporary bankers. It serves to concentrate their attention on the relations between developed-creditor nations and developing-debtor nations. The very uncertainty imposed on both borrowers and lenders as endless debt reschedulings proceed argues powerfully for longer-term and more rational reconstruction.

In sum, countries argue that the margins they pay on loans are too high; fees banks charge for rescheduling debts too steep; and U.S. interest rates to which most developing country loans are pegged are suffocatingly high. Moreover, maturities on rescheduled loans are too short and not enough new financing has been forthcoming from either commercial bankers or their governments. Furthermore, the IMF's adjustment programs impose unacceptable social and financial burdens on debtor countries while growing protectionism in industrial countries makes it very difficult for developing countries to export their way out of debt. Finally, the major developed-creditor countries failed to maintain monetary stability, thus exacerbating the already serious problems of the 1970s and making difficult the integration of developing-debtor countries into the world economy.

It is unlikely that debtor countries will form a debtor's cartel as envisioned by such outspoken debtor countries as Venezuela, Ecuador, and Bolivia. Mexico, for instance, has come a long way toward making internal policy changes and restructuring its obligations. The same is true of Yugoslavia and other countries. The driving force to the debtor cartel idea apparently is given by people who view the international economy as structurally biased against developing countries. The net effect of such discussions, however, may well be to frighten off the smaller U.S. and European banks from international lending and continuing partnership with large world banks, thereby leaving the debtor nations in an even worse situation. It is, in effect, a strategy that runs counter to our theory of cooperation.

It is equally important, moreover, not to overstate the consequences of default. To be sure there would be a decline in world trade. Trade among most countries, however, would decline marginally. Trade with defaulting countries would not be reduced to zero. Various arrangements, including financial, would continue to be made with a defaulted country. Some arrangements, moreover, would become more attractive since the defaulted country would no longer have an outstanding debt to worry about. There would also be an increase in barter and countertrade arrangements. In 1983, for instance, GATT attributed a maximum of 5 percent of world trade to countertrade, or roughly $40 billion a year.

In fact, the increased popularity of barter and countertrade owes much of their new vitality to the world's monetary and debt problems. It appeals almost equally to developing countries short of cash and to the international banks wary of extending them credit. Barter periodically stages a comeback when major political or economic developments undermine the world's trading system. So it was in the 1970s after the sharp oil price rises. Banks shaken by Latin American and other developing-debtor countries' debt debacle are discovering barter's attractions anew.

In addition to barter, the main types of countertrade are counter-purchase, buy-back, and bilateral trade. Under classical barter arrangements, goods are directly exchanged in a single contract. The pure barter method is no longer common today.

Counter-purchase, on the other hand, has become increasingly popular. It is also complex. Under this system, an exporter signs a letter of intent pledging to buy goods from the importing country. This method often entails the involvement of a third party, such as the countertrade department of a bank or trading company, which assumes the exporter's obligation.

Buy-back, more common than barter, is now an increasing practice. Accordingly, products that are traded form the pay-off for one of the parties. Thus the Germans participating in construction of the Soviet gas pipeline will be repaid with Soviet natural gas.

Counterpurchase increasingly is coming under government legislation. In fact, such countries as Argentina, Mexico, and others with debt problems now insist on counterpurchase as a part of any trade agreement. OPEC has been particularly important in encouraging counterpurchase and countertrade arrangements as a way of trying to shore up oil prices.

Countertrade is inefficient and costly. It distorts trade patterns. Money is simply a more efficient means of financing trade. It is not, however, something you do because you want to do it. You do it because you do not have enough "money" in your account to do otherwise. Typically, countertrade is a short-term solution for developing countries' lack of cash and marketing skills.

Finally, default would bring about contractions in some sectors of the world's market economies and expansions in other sectors. Thus if international trade declines, the resources employed in export sectors will eventually rise to produce goods and services formerly imported or their close substitutes. This is, in effect, the manner in which a new equilibrium is worked out. It is not likely that the new equilibrium thus attained will be superior to the pre-default position.

It is becoming increasingly clear that the IMF is still trying to deal with the problems of developing-debtor countries with some very old-fashioned methods. What was a suitable policy prescription for a relatively rich developed country attempting to hold a fixed parity for its exchange rate under the postwar Bretton Woods System is not suitable for poor countries facing proportionately more pressing problems and with populations at appallingly low levels of income. Very real hardships can result with serious political consequences for the entire world. The second problem is that indebtedness and hence recourse to the IMF is too widespread after the oil shocks of the 1970s for the aggregate of individual deals between the IMF and particular countries not to have a depressing effect on world trade.

It may be that the third world debt of almost $700 billion owed to world banks and governments of developed creditor-nations can be reduced in the medium term at some considerable economic and political cost to the developing debtor nations accompanied by a buoyant world recovery. There are, however, significant risks in any such course. One major world bank (Morgan Guaranty Trust) calculates that a growth rate of 3 percent a year in the OECD countries, with interest rates declining to 3 percent in real terms, would still leave the 21 largest borrowers with a ratio of debt to exports of 123 percent by 1990, compared with 178 percent in 1982. Some consider this scenario as optimistic; each 1-percent drop in the industrial countries' average growth would reduce developing-debtor nations' world earnings by $11 billion a year, with each 1-percent point rise in interest rates costing them an extra $4 billion. Even with a favorable world economy, very real risks exist that a developing-debtor country would suffer such economic hardship and political instability that it would declare a moratorium on its debts and that the developed-creditor nations' banks would consequently lose the confidence of their customers, freeze their lending and abruptly disrupt world trade. The collapse of one part of the world banking system would not leave the whole intact given the interdependence of the world system.

Many people now feel that much more is required of the IMF than a mere increase in quotas, some relaxations of its conditions, or an issue of Special Drawing Rights, effectively world currency which IMF members can use to fund current account deficits. All of those changes at the margin may well be necessary just to continue the process of muddling through and hoping for the best.

Congressman Jack Kemp (R. N.Y.), for instance, calls for a conference similar to Bretton Woods to reform the international monetary system to bring about a more liberal trade climate.[5] IMF policy restrictions must be reordered, according to Congressman Kemp, from austerity to growth and maintained with strict guidelines. Conditionality should include lower tax rates on labor and capital in recognition that austerity is not the problem of developing nations. It is the problem.[6] In effect, finance ministers of developing-debtor countries should be forewarned that any additional funding of the IMF should be used to fund economic reform rather than merely more of the same policies that led to the crisis that additional funding is now presuambly to solve.

There is no shortage of proposed solutions as we have discussed. Some call for an extension of export credit agencies to cover bank lending. Others would reconstruct maturities, provide guarantees of repayment, or tie fresh lending to World Bank projects and criteria. Not all meet the two desirable criteria from the standpoint of debtors and creditors, that no excessive costs should be imposed on borrowers since they were led, presumably, to acquire the debt during the 1970s as much by the encouragement of laissez-faire recycling by the West's authorities as by anyone else, and that lenders have an incentive to continue lending, rather than retrench as their market instincts tell them to do so that the process of adjustment can be allowed time.

Our theory of cooperation based on reciprocity and incorporating a Tit for Tat strategy does provide guildelines for a long-run solution consistent with these criteria. It has the added virtue that it is simple. We have discussed one method for implementing our theory. These are technicalities, however, and other methods come to mind.

For instance, some methods could incorporate Mr. Kemp's suggestion that the IMF place emphasis on incentives and economic growth rather than austerity as a condition of loans to troubled countries. They could also include some pain for banks, since they bet on inflation and lost. Bankers could also be required to write down some loans so that their balance sheets reflect more fact and less fiction. The methods could also be constructed to eliminate "debtor-leverage". In any case the methods most likely to be effective will incorporate less regulation and more market discipline.

Essential to an evolving environment of cooperation and reciprocity is domestic and international monetary stability. Monetary authorities and central bankers must ensure that the monetary system itself is not a source of world instability. They must also provide an elastic currency so as to keep the money supply from contracting in the event of a run on their banks.

ROLE FOR MONEY AND MONETARY POLICY

This does not mean accommodating banks and debtor countries because they guessed wrong on inflation. Nor does it mean depending on the wisdom of central bankers and international bureaucrats to diagnose and prescribe for monetary policy. Neither is consistent with our theory of cooperation. Consistent with our theory is a policy system based on rules and nondiscretionary intervention into the economy. Its policy corollary is that only a slow and steady rate of increase in the money supply — one in line with the real growth of the economy — can ensure price stability.[7]

This is essentially the Monetarist position. It contrasts with the views of central bankers and others whose preference is administrative discretionary intervention to maintain aggregate demand in the economy. Consistent with their view is that monetary policy is an art not to be encumbered by explicit policy rules. This is, in effect, a "central bank monetary standard." Who can predict the future value of the dollar, pound, mark, or yen on the basis of a central bank standard?

Consistent with our theory and an evolving environment of cooperation and reciprocity on the domestic and international levels would be a fiduciary monetary standard within a "monetary constitution." This is essentially a Monetarist proposal. It is suggested by Leland Yeager and James Buchanan and incorporates a Friedman type rule on the rate of monetary growth.[8] On the international level, fully flexible exchange rates would replace the existing "dirty-float" system of exchange rates.

One merit of these proposals for constraining the monetary system by a monetary constitution and rule is their implicit recognition that the nineteenth century integration of market processes has been impaired over the past several decades by the emergence in every country of a greater measure of state intervention in the monetary sphere. Moreover, the degree of intervention varies from complete central planning such as in the Soviet Union and other East European countries through various modifications of the social service state to national economies still operating for the most part on a basis of private enterprise.

The fact is that in every country there has been an increased degree of intervention, and in all, the instruments of intervention, for the most part, are national. The flexibility of exchange rates could well deputize for the varying degrees of price flexibility in internal price structures brought about by state intervention. Such a flexible system also takes into account varying political, economic, cultural, and indeed industrial conditions of the world community of nations, thereby avoiding conflict over sensitive issues of national sovereignty. The IMF has never become the constraining influence on national monetary systems, nor the international central bank that some of its founders hoped it would.

Other proposals would also be consistent with our theory, though they lack the support they once had. For instance, recent proposals for return to some form of the gold standard as a constraint on the domestic and international monetary system have not met with notable success.[9] This is not surprising. What is often lacking in these proposals is an appreciation and understanding of the fact that the gold standard was more than a monetary standard. It cannot be understood, as it can not be operated successfully except as part of a socioeconomic, political, and philosophic system in which it was developed. This system no longer exists.

There is, moreover, a tendency on the part of some gold standard advocates to overlook some of its more troublesome aspects. Thus between 1815 and 1914 there were 12 major crises or panics in the United States which pushed up interest rates, created severe unemployment, and suspended specie payments (conversion of the dollar into gold) in addition to 14 more minor recessions.[10] To be sure, between 1879 and 1965 a period when America was on some sort of gold standard (the dollar's final links with gold were not cut until 1971 during President Nixon's administration), the consumer price index rose by an average of only 1.4 percent a year. On the other hand, the severe bouts of inflation were followed by deep deflation in which prices actually fell. For instance, in the 1921 world recession when production actually fell for only a few months, there were 30-40 percent cuts in manufacturing wages in some countries in the period 1920-22.

An alternative proposal, pushed from theory to practice by F. A. Hayek, is that governmental monopoly in the supply of money be abolished and that the provision of money be left to an unregulated market.[11] Hayek contends that with private provision of money, money users would receive a better product, and the problems of business cycles would be alleviated. Pre-1860 American monetary experience with multiple private currencies, which I examine elsewhere, sheds light on the feasibility of Hayek's proposal.[12] At that time, moreover, the ultimate constraint on the American monetary system was the specie or gold standard. Hayek's proposal on this score is not clear.

Money is an idea which in good measure embodies civilization. It is a link between past, present, and future. The extension and use of national money to the international economy is similar to the extension of the gains from free trade and self-realization to the world stage. As a result money and its stability is a source of controversies. These controversies have important implications for our theory of cooperation and a strategy of Tit for Tat. Consider, briefly, these controversies.

Classical and neoclassical economists promoted the rules of the gold or specie standard as a means for constraining the international and domestic monetary systems within bounds so as to minimize the chances that money would become a political issue and a source of instability. Even so, they were not always successful. The system's periodic breakdown provides ample testimony on this score.

The nineteenth century view of society's responsibility to maintain trust and faith in money was supported by the bitter eighteenth century experiences with monetary manipulation and currency excess. Most classical economists and certainly the "Austrians" underscored society's monetary responsibilities for preserving trust and faith in money. The spirit of the tradition is against the use of discretionary monetary policy for the purpose of exploiting the presumed, short-run nonneutrality of money in order to increase permanently employment and output by increasing the stock of money. Though an arbitrary increase in money, in their view, will not necessarily disrupt relative-prices permanently, such manipulation sets into motion forces the consequences of which for social stability are very serious indeed. Since no human power can guarantee against possible misuse of money-issuing authority, to give such unconstrained authority to government is to invite destruction of the social order. To avoid such temptation it is best to tie paper money to a metal value established by law or the economy.[13]

The use of discretionary policy to exploit the short-run non-neutrality of money is a good illustration of a counterproductive non-nice strategy incompatible with our theory of cooperation. Indeed, its tertiary effect is to compromise the monetary authority's credibility thereby destroying the very environment upon which its success depends. In the process the monetary system itself is cast in doubt.

This does not mean that government intervention per se into the economy and specifically into monetary affairs is somehow peculiar to the twentieth century. On the contrary, as we noted, many classical and neoclassical economists devoted considerable effort to the definition of international and domestic monetary systems under which total demand would behave "appropriately". They recognized the optional and political determination of the country's monetary system and the need to constrain it with policy based on rules.

It was J. M. Keynes who made the revolt against the predominant view of money respectable. It was George Simmel and others long before Keynes who first suggested the sources of the revolt and foresaw its likely consequences. They did not see the institution of money in mechanical terms but as a conflict between abstract concepts of money and the social trust on which it rests. Their concern was to elucidate the moral basis of monetary order in contrast to the subversion of morals through money, in the abstract, which was feared. Many were pessimistic that the traditional monetary order would survive the revolt against it. On this score they were not to be disappointed.

Keynes, too, was concerned with monetary stability and the fragile nature of a money-using market economy and the social order that went with it.[14] He was also well aware of the need for trust in the stability of purchasing power if the market mechanism was to function properly. Indeed, to Keynes money is not just another commodity. A money economy is very different from a barter economy. This idea was lost, write Laidler and Rowe, as the Hicksian IS-LM interpretation of the *General Theory* came to dominate monetary economics, "monetarist" as well as so-called 'Keynesian'. The dominance of this incomplete version of Keynes in subsequent debates has also surely been the main reason for participants in them having neglected 'Austrian' ideas on these matters. . . .[15]

The story, however, is very different on the conduct of monetary policy where Keynes and his followers depart significantly from the Austrian and Monetarist paths. These differences are so profound as to overwhelm areas of agreement. As we have had occasion to note elsewhere, Keynes believed firmly in discretionary monetary policy and viewed the gold standard as a relic. Modern Austrians and some supply-siders hold to the gold-standard. Monetarists argue for a given growth rate in the stock of money. The difference between the Austrians and Monetarists is essentially about means to achieve agreed-upon ends. The Austrians, while distrusting bureaucrats, are more skeptical than Monetarists about the stability of the demand for money function and so opt for pegging the price of money in terms of gold relying on the stability of the relative price of gold in terms of goods in general.

The essence of monetarism then is that money matters a great deal, that it is a key determinant of short-term economic trends. If the money supply behaves erratically so does the economy. Most economists can accept monetarism in those simple terms. The differences arise, as we noted, when we turn to policy prescription.

To the nonmonetarist the fact that money matters means that it is something to be carefully manipulated by the central bank through discretionary intervention. In the short-run, faster money growth is likely to produce lower interest rates. If the objective is lower interest rates, simply speed up the money supply. This also means that banks are using increased reserves to make loans to people. If the objective is increased economic activity, speed up money growth.

It is agreed that typically fast money growth within a year or two can mean higher prices, so it is important to know when to slow money growth. The trouble with this approach, according to the Monetarists, is that we really do not know when to slow money's growth. For one thing, the lags between changes in the money supply growth and the economy are varied and unpredictable. For another, an attempt to fine-tune monetary policy is likely to cause more problems than it solves.

Given such an environment the best the government can do, continue the Monetarists, is to promote steady growth of the money supply at a moderate rate. This rate is roughly equal to the economy's capacity to grow. For the money supply, the Fed as well as other Central Banks use M1 (currency plus checking deposits).[16] Concern over "what-is-money" arguments has also prompted the use of monetary base (currency plus bank reserves) or merely bank reserves as central bank money supply targets. A policy of stable monetary growth would remove money from the political arena and as a source of economic instability.

To be sure neither the Federal Reserve, nor other central banks, is "Monetarist" in the sense that Friedman and other Monetarists would like. The differences, however, have narrowed somewhat in the past three or four years. They now turn mostly but not completely on the execution of policy. For example, the slow down in monetary growth carried out by many of the central banks has been erratic and uneven. In the case of the Fed, making a few technical adjustments would presumably get it on the right track. For instance, under current practice, required reserves are determined by the level of their deposits two weeks earlier thereby placing the initiative for monetary policy in the hands of banks. In February 1984 the Fed will switch to a system tying requirements to the deposits of two days earlier. This should improve matters.

Some nonmonetarists and antimonetarists, on the other hand, are saying that we should leave money and monetary policy up to the wisdom of the Federal Reserve System. The Fed would go back to trying to police interest rates, although the Fed seems to recognize now that its power to control rates is very limited. The Fed would keep an eye on everything and do the very best it could.

That surely adds up to much more discretionary administrative intervention by the Fed, if only because the central bank would have so many accidental errors to try to correct. That does not fit well with what the Reagan administration has been trying to do — namely, lessen the government's role in the lives of its citizens. It is certainly inconsistent with the views of Monetarists and others seeking lawful policy systems and limitations on the undefined exercise of power by government.

It is, however, appealing to central bankers and consistent with the modern Keynesian approach and discretionary economic intervention without defined guides or policy systems as we have discussed.

Money is thus pushed into the political arena to be fought over according to one's ideological and philosophic inclinations. The idea promoted by Keynesians and others is that money and monetary institutions are simply creations of the state and thus available for manipulation by government, consisting, for the most part, of wise and well-educated people disinterestedly promoting the best interests of society. In essence, it is at best an elitist view of government or at worst a totalitarian government.

It is also characteristic of the type of discretionary interventionism which has grown rapidly since the Keynesian revolution, although it began long before Keynes as I have discussed elsewhere.[17] The fact is, for several decades now we have been witnessing a conflict between two incompatible concepts of money: money as a tool of the state and money as a symbol of social trust.[18]

The traditional view of money focused on a monetary order that implied a nondiscretionary policy ordered system whose operation would not be arbitrarily altered by discretionary intervention in favor of particular individuals, groups, or interests. The survival of such a monetary order has long been questioned by some for the reason that it might not prove possible to make it work in terms of specific goals that society should, in their opinion, pursue. This view, shared by J. M. Keynes, leads to utopian attempts to make the uncertain certain by control of society according to plan as well as by transformation of man.

To use the monetary system to pursue changing goals and objectives is incompatible with a stable monetary order. It will make it "capricious and uncertain and prey to conflicting and varying political objectives."[19] A monetary policy, writes Frankel, "which is directed to shifting goals — as for example, full employment, economic growth, economic equality or the attempt to satisfy conflicting demands of capital and labour — cannot but vary with the goals adopted."[20] Friedman sums up the issue well as we cited in that "We are in danger of assigning to monetary policy a larger role than it can perform in danger of asking it to accomplish tasks that it cannot achieve and, as a result, in danger of preventing it from making the contribution that it is capable of making. . . ."[21] Intended to reduce uncertainty, monetary manipulation thus actually increases it by casting doubt on the monetary system itself. This is well illustrated in a number of American historical and contemporary episodes upon which this book draws.

A BRETTON WOODS II?

There is a simmering debate on calling a Bretton Woods II Conference to consider, among other issues, what changes in the world's monetary system can be made to ease the global debt problem. Should the world try to revive the fixed exchange system — or should it possibly return to a gold standard?

To some the idea of a Bretton Woods II conference is tempting to return to the serenity of a system of fixed exchange. To others a second Bretton Woods conference would be a nightmare. At the 1944 conference, only 44 countries were represented; today, a truly global monetary conference would require invitations to 162 countries, with many clamoring for an equal vote with the major industrial nations.

The current system of floating exchange rates (or *dirty float*) has plenty of critics.[22] They argue that short-term fluctuations often lead to longer-term misalignments of currencies making U.S. goods more expensive — and hence less competitive abroad. As a result, the critics contend, businesses tend to shun export markets, world trade is depressed and the debt problems of the poorer countries grow worse.

Memories on some matters tend to be short for it is not at all clear that a system of fixed exchange rates would operate any better under current world conditions characterized by widely varying inflation rates and heavy international capital flows. As a matter of fact, the Bretton Woods system of fixed exchange rates worked for less than a decade. It really came into full operation in 1958 when the major European countries finally agreed to make their currency freely convertible into dollars. It began to fall apart in the late 1960s when the British pound came under heavy pressure as a consequence of internal economic difficulties. Moreover, frequent crises dominated the system as governments sought vainly to defend unrealistic exchange rates. These contests, moreover, were generally won by the markets and lost by central banks.

The collapse of the Bretton Woods agreement was brought about by a combination of circumstances. Accelerating inflation in the United States, regained economic strength by Europe and Japan, coupled with large capital flows and an exchange rate which had not been changed since World War II, placed pressure on the American dollar. The system's end came in 1971, as we noted, when President Nixon convinced that the run on the dollar was reaching alarming proportions, ordered the closing of the gold window. After months of last ditch efforts to set new fixed exchange rates, the world officially turned to floating exchange rates in March 1973. For some countries attempts to maintain a fixed parity turned out to be very expensive indeed. Germany's central bank, for instance, lost $10 billion in 1983 prices in a fruitless attempt to maintain parity between the mark and the dollar.

It was expected that a system of floating exchange rates would put to rest problems which plagued the fixed exchange rate system of Bretton Woods. Henceforth markets would set exchange rates. The system would be self-correcting.

In practice, however, it turned out that the world was not on a freely floating or fully flexible exchange rate system as envisioned by theory. Some of the constraints that had served as benchmarks and put pressure on governments to adjust their economic policies when their exchange rates were out of line were removed. By maintaining a low valued yen, Japan, for instance, increased the competitiveness of its goods and services while protecting itself from high unemployment. In effect, the freedom to ignore the pre-1971 rules has become the freedom to devalue, to inflate, and to exclude foreign competition from home markets. As a result the world economy is unlikely to return to the high growth rates of the 1950s and 1960s.

Given the turbulent years of the 1970s however, the floating rate system has performed reasonably well. There is very little evidence that the system of floating exchange rates has caused more inflation or reduced the volume of world trade. Rather than abandon the system, some critics would opt for more intervention by government in foreign exchange markets. Such intervention would presumably send a signal by the authorities to the speculators when the latter have pushed the currency too far.

Intervention, however, appears to be a useless exercise given disparities among national inflation rates. The markets usually win these games at considerable cost to intervening central banks and monetary authorities. Once inflation is brought down and under control the existing system will become less volatile.

Intervention, moreover, can be seen as a substitute for policy. Dollar creation, whether by the Federal Reserve or foreign desk, is still dollar creation. The Reagan administration has for the most part resisted pressures from abroad to create dollars as a way of making other currencies look stronger in the exchange markets. To a degree, this policy has had its source in Beryl Sprinkel's Monetarist views which dictate that a currency float should be a real float with no market-distorting interventions. There is a more practical reason as well. If you do not intervene, other nations that want to keep their currencies on a par have only one option available, pursuit of sound economic policies. In short, the United States can unilaterally apply discipline to the world economy and save the world a lot of inflationary grief, restoring something approximating the old Bretton Woods system that was based on a strong gold-linked dollar.

Politicians, of course, resist monetary discipline, which is why Bretton Woods broke down. And politicians, both in the United States and abroad, are resisting unilateral dollar discipline that the administration has been trying to enforce. The U.S. Congress has refused to bring the growth in federal spending down. The Germans and the French, to name but two examples out of many, are fretting about the reluctance of investors to put their money in marks and francs when those currencies look so shakey vis-à-vis the dollar, ignoring the possibility that what the investors are worried about has more to do with Germany's Ostpolitik and France's socialism than with any fault in U.S. dollar policy. Intervention in the foreign exchange markets may show U.S. good will, but no amount of it will change these fundamentals. Such a strategy does not promote long lasting cooperation as envisioned by our theory. Indeed, the contrary is more likely to be the end result.

Recent compromise proposals by some economists (for example, Ronald McKinnon) would establish *target zones* for the dollar, yen, and mark. The United States, Japan and Germany then would pledge to keep their currency values within those values. This would require considerable coordination among the three countries. Their monetary and fiscal policies would have to be aimed at maintaining the agreed-upon exchange rates. They would also be obliged, when necessary, to intervene in the exchange markets to maintain their rates.

Critics argue that such an arrangement has too many of the disadvantages of floating exchange rates and too many of the burdens of the fixed exchange rate system. In fact, the governments would also be required to set target zones for inflation and for real interest rates as well. If they could accomplish all of this there would be no need for an exchange-rate target since the exchange rates themselves would be stable.

It is unclear how far the post-1983 Williamsburg negotiations will go toward overhauling the present system. France and Italy are pushing for a return to a fixed-rate system. The U.S. program on the other hand calls for preserving the existing system and a wait-and-see attitude. Britain and Germany tend to agree with the U.S. view. American preference is to examine the role of existing international institutions such as the Bank for International Settlements (established, as we discussed, to deal with German reparation payments) in handling the international debt problem.

Indeed there is increasing pressure, notable from debt burdened commercial banks, for the BIS to become a more permanent lender of last resort to debt-ridden countries, similar to the role now played by the IMF. In fact, a group of private banks negotiating a $1.1 billion loan to Argentina in 1982 even made approval of a loan from BIS or the Federal Reserve System a condition for granting that country new loans.

It is true that the BIS has been moving in the direction of becoming an agency for organizing central banks in an interim role in managing the current global debt problem. It has also played a gradually increasing role in the international monetary system. As a forum for central bankers, BIS has often been in the forefront of significant new policy decisions. Though technically a privately held bank, the BIS also manages the European monetary system. And it gathers considerable economic intelligence.

For its part, however, the BIS does not wish to become a lender of last resort if that means bailing out debt-plagued countries despite recent loans to Mexico, Brazil, and Yugoslavia. For one thing, it is not equipped to provide medium-term or long-term loans even though its balance sheet in 1982 totalled $40 billion. The reason is that its central bank clients must be able to pull out their deposits at a moment's notice and the bank's own investments are all short-term. To lend to countries for more than a short period is thus out of the question. Furthermore, the bank lacks the staff to monitor and carry out extensive loan operations, for example, it has a staff of about 300 compared to the IMF's 2500; nor does it have the power to require countries to adopt austerity measures as a condition for a loan.

Currently, the BIS has three criteria for its lending: the loans must be used as short-term financing until another source of financing comes through; they must be backed by collateral; they must be linked to some form of automatic repayment, for instance, a pending IMF loan. This provides the bank with considerable flexibility. As a result it is able very quickly to put together a short-term loan without burdensome investigation.

Despite Washington's reluctance, some observers believe that a new international monetary conference is inevitable, even though it may be a few years away. If so, the advice of our theory of cooperation should serve as a guide to the participants: Do not be envious, do not be the first to defect, reciprocate both defection and cooperation, and do not be too clever. The studies and techniques we have discussed for promoting cooperation in an iterated Prisoner's Dilemma might also be useful to a Bretton Woods II conference as well as to ongoing attempts to amicably and satisfactorily resolve the current world debt issue.

NOTES

1. See J. C. Riley, *International Government Finance and the Amsterdam Capital Market, 1740-1845* (New York and Cambridge: Cambridge University Press, 1980).

2. For a discussion regarding such a cartel see "Latin Debtors Try Shaking the Money Tree Again," *Business Week*, September 12, 1983, pp. 108-10.

3. See, for instance, J. Eaton and M. Gersovitz, "Debt for Potential Repudiation: Theoretical and Empirical Analysis," *Review of Economic Studies*, April 1981, pp. 289-309; J. Sachs, "LDC Debt in the 1980's: Risk and Reform," NBER Working Paper No. 861, February, 1982; J. Sadis and Daniel Cohen, "LDC Borrowing With Default Risk," NBER Working Paper No. 925, July 1982; M. Cooley and P. Isard, "Country Risk, International Lending, and Exchange Rate Determination," *International Finance Discussion Papers* No. 221, May 10, 1983.

4. See, for instance, George Macesich, *Politics of Monetarism: Its Historical and Institutional Development* (Totowa, N.J.: Littlefield and Adams, 1984).

5. Jack Kemp, "The Solution to World Debt is World Growth," *The Wall Street Journal*, February 10, 1983, p. 30.

6. See John Williams, "On Seeking to Improve IMF Conditionality," *The American Economic Review*, May 1983, pp. 354-58; John Williams, *The Lending Policies of the International Monetary Fund* (Washington: Institute for International Economics, 1982); John Williams, *IMF Conditionality* (Washington:

Institute for International Economics, 1983); L. T. Katseli, "Devaluation: A Critical Appraisal of the I.M.F.'s Policy Prescriptions," *The American Economic Review*, May 1, 1983, pp. 359-63.

7. See, for instance, Milton Friedman, "The Role of Monetary Policy" in *The Optimum Quantity of Money and Other Essays* Milton Friedman, ed. (Chicago: Aldine, 1969), p. 99. See also George Macesich, *Monetarism: Theory and Policy* (New York: Praeger Publishers, 1983); George Macesich, *The Politics of Monetarism: Its Historical and Institutional Development* (Totowa, N.J.: Littlefield and Adams, 1984), for discussion of a number of these ideas as well as bibliography; George Macesich, *World Crises and Developing Countries* (Belgrade: Informator, 1984).

8. See, for example, Leland B. Yeager (ed.), *In Search of a Monetary Constitution* (Cambridge: Harvard University Press, 1962); James Buchanan, "Predictability: The Criterion of Monetary Constitutions," in ibid., pp. 155-83; Milton Friedman, "Should There Be an Independent Monetary Authority?" in ibid, pp. 219-43; Milton Friedman and Anna J. Schwartz, *A Monetary History of the United States 1867-1960* (Princeton: Princeton University Press, 1963); Milton Friedman, *A Program for Monetary Stability* (New York: Fordham University Press, 1959). See also Robert E. Lucas, Jr., "Rules, Discretion, and the Role of Economic Advisor," in S. Fischer (ed.), *Rational Expectations and Economic Policy* (Chicago: University of Chicago Press, 1980), pp. 199-210; T. J. Sargent and N. Wallace, "Rational Expectations, the Optimal Monetary Instrument, and the Optimal Money Supply Rule," *Journal of Political Economy* 83, 1975, pp. 241-54; George Macesich, *The Politics of Monetarism: Its Historical and Institutional Development*, Chs. 1 and 8.

9. See, for example, a useful summary by M. D. Bordo, "The Classical Gold Standard: Some Lessons for Today," *Review, Federal Reserve Bank of St. Louis*, May 1981, pp. 1-16; R. M. Bleiberg and J. Grant, "For Real Money: The Dollar Should Be As Good As Gold," editorial commentary, *Barron's*, June 15, 1981; L. E. Lehrman and Henry S. Reuss (debate), "Should the U.S. Return to the Gold Standard?" *Christian Science Monitor*, September 21, 1981; *The Economist*, September 5, 1981, pp. 11-12, the report of the U.S. Gold Commission studying greater role for gold in U.S.; see also Martin Bronfenbrenner, "The Currency-Choice Defense," *Challenge*, January/February 1980, pp. 31-36: "The gold clause was relegalized by Section 463 of the U.S. Code in October 1977. Little publicity has been accorded this change; few people know about it; any rush of gold clauses may lead Congress to reverse its 1977 action. On the other hand, that action may be a straw in the wind; it has friends in Congress; extension of the legal tender privilege to other currencies and thus freer competition between currencies may be closer in the U.S. market than anyone realizes" (p. 36). See also Anna J. Schwartz, "The U.S. Gold Commission and the Resurgence of Interest in A Return to the Gold Standard," *Proceedings and Reports* Vol. 17, 1983 (Tallahassee: Center for Yugoslav-American Studies, Research and Exchanges, Florida State University, 1983). Dr. Schwartz was the Executive Director of the U.S. Gold Commission; George Macesich, *The Politics of Monetarism: Its Historical and Institutional Development*, op. cit., chs. 1 and 8.

10. *The Economist*, September 19, 1981, pp. 17-18.

11. F. A. Hayek, *Denationalization of Money* (London: Institute of Economic Affairs, 1976).

12. George Macesich, *The Politics of Monetarism: Its Historical and Institutional Development*, ch. 8.

13. This was a view widely shared. For instance, Georg Simmel a German sociologist in an important but often overlooked study *The Philosophy of Money* first published in 1907 in Berlin (*Philosophie des Geldes*), writes, ". . . The most serious repercussions upon exchange transactions will follow from this situation, particularly at the moment when the government's own resources are paid in devalued money. The numerator of the money fraction — the price of commodities — rises proportionately to the increased supply of money only after large quantities of new money have already been spent by the government, which then finds itself confronted again with a redeemed supply of money. The temptation then to make a new issue of money is generally irresistible and the process begins all over again. I mention this only as example of the numerous and frequently discussed failures of arbitrary issues of paper money, which present themselves as a temptation whenever money is not closely linked with a substance of limited supply. . . . Today we know that only precious metals, and indeed only gold, guarantee the requisite qualities, and in particular the limitation of quantity; and that paper money can escape the dangers of misuse by arbitrary inflation, only if it is tied to metal value established by law or by the economy. . . ." Georg Simmel, *The Philosophy of Money*, translation by T. Bottomore and D. Frisby, with Introduction by D. Frisby (London and Boston: Routledge and Kegan Paul, 1977), p. 160. See also David Laidler and Nicholas Rowe, "Georg Simmel's *Philosophy of Money*: A review article for Economists," *Journal of Economic Literature*, March, 1980, pp. 97-105.

14. See Laidler and Rowe, op. cit., p. 103.

15. Ibid.

16. For a detailed analysis of definitions of the money supply see Milton Friedman and Anna J. Schwartz, *Monetary Statistics of the United States* (New York: Columbia University Press for National Bureau of Economic Research, 1970).

17. George Macesich, *The Politics of Monetarism*.

18. See S. Herbert Frankel, *Two Philosophies of Money: The Conflict of Trust and Authority* (New York: St. Martin's Press, 1977), p. 86; and George Macesich, *The International Monetary Economy and the Third World* (New York: Praeger Publishers, 1981), ch. 1.

19. Frankel, op. cit., p. 89.

20. Ibid., p. 92.

21. Milton Friedman, "The Role of Monetary Policy," in *The Optiminum Quantity of Money and Other Essays* Milton Friedman, ed. (Chicago: Aldine, 1969), p. 99.

22. See for instance the discussions in R. N. Cooper et al. (eds.), *The International Monetary System under Flexible Exchange Rates: Global Regional and National: Essays in Honor of Robert Triffin* (Cambridge, Mass.: Harper & Row, Ballinger, 1982); Betty C. Daniel, "The International Transmission of Economic

Disturbances under Flexible Exchange Rates," *International Economic Review*, October 1981, pp. 491-509; Ronald Findlay and Carlos Rodrigues, "Intermediate Imports and Macroeconomic Policy under Flexible Exchange Rates," *The Canadian Journal of Economics* May 1977, pp. 208-17; Koichi Hamada, "Alternative Exchange Rate Systems and the Interdependence of Monetary Policies," in *National Monetary Policies and the International Financial System*, Robert Z. Aliber, ed. (Chicago: University of Chicago Press, 1974); Koichi Hamada, "A Strategic Analysis of Monetary Interdependence," *Journal of Political Economy* August 1976, pp. 677-700; Koichi Hamada, "Macroeconomic Strategy Coordination under Alternative Exchange Rates," in *International Economic Policy*, Rudiger Dornbusch and Jacob Frenkel, eds. (Baltimore: Johns Hopkins University Press, 1979); Koichi Hamada and Sakurai Makoto, "International Transmission of Stagflation under Fixed and Flexible Exchange Rates," *Journal of Political Economy* October 1978, pp. 877-96; Dale Henderson, "Financial Policies in Open Economies," *American Economic Review* May 1979, pp. 232-39; Michael Jones, "Automatic Output Stability and the Exchange Arrangement: A Multi-Country Analysis," *Review of Economic Studies* Vol. 69, 1982a, pp. 91-107; Robert A. Mundell, "Capital Mobility and Stabilization Policy under Fixed and Flexible Exchange Rates," *Canadian Journal of Economics and Political Science*, November, 1963, pp. 475-85; Michael Mussa, "Macroeconomic Interdependence and the Exchange Rate Regime," in *International Economic Policy: Theory and Evidence*, Rudiger Dornbusch and Jacob Frenkel, eds. (Baltimore: The Johns Hopkins University Press, 1979); Jeffry Sachs, "Energy and Growth under Flexible Exchange Rates: A Simulation Study," NBER Working Paper No. 582 (November 1980).

INDEX

ABOUT THE AUTHOR

GEORGE MACESICH is professor of Economics and Director of the Center for Yugoslav-American Studies, Research and Exchanges at the Florida State University in Tallahassee. He received his Ph.D. in economics from the University of Chicago. His books, among others, include *The International Monetary Economy and the Third World*; with R. Lang and D. Vojnić (eds.), *Essays on the Political Economy of Yugoslavia*; with Hui-Liang Tsai, *Money in Economic Systems*; *Monetarism: Theory and Policy.*; with D. Dimitrijević, *Money and Finance in Yugoslavia: A Comparative Analysis*; *The Politics of Monetarism: Its Historical and Institutional Development*; *World Crisis and Developing Countries*; and *Banking and Third World Debt: In Search of Solutions*.